Thanks for your Support! Pray for Snow.

Sincerely,

Jason Hummel

MT. BAKER, COLEMAN GLACIER

Josh Hummel skis between crevasses. He's chased by a pocket slab toward golden slopes above the Salish Sea.

Table of Contents

Alpine State Of Mind - VOLUME 1
By Jason Hummel. Design by Scott Hollis.
Printed in Canada. All rights reserved. Copyright © 2015 Jason Hummel.
Reproduction without permission is prohibited.
To order hard copies, go to www.AlpineStateofMindJournal.com
Send correspondence to alpinestateofmind@gmail.com
On the front cover: Adam Roberts on the North Face, Northwest Ridge of Mt. Adams, South
Cascades, Washington State. **On the back cover:** Kyle Miller and Ben Starkey skinning up the
north side of Mount Rainier. Mount Rainier National Park, Washington State.

Where It All Began

The Inspiration

When I decided to write this book, I thought it would come together effortlessly. How misguided I was! It reminds me of how so many mountain adventures have began. I recall myself convincing partners, "The weather is perfect. The snow is deep. It'll be no problem, and (contrary to the forecast) we have plenty of time before the storm rolls in." Like any great trip, putting this book together has tested my limits and pushed me out of my comfort zone.

Three stories are highlighted in Volume One, which showcases ski mountaineering. Other editions will include additional sports, but for now I share stories of snow, the white gold that is precious to so many of us.

The first story is about the American Alps Traverse. This 16-day ski trip along the backbone of the North Cascades was a dream trip and the culmination of a lifetime of adventure in my home mountain range. A grin spreads over my face whenever I think of it. Many of the adventures I've had since I was a child intersect and are tied together by this venture. While merely 120 miles and 60,000 feet of vertical gain and loss, there was a weight to every mile and every foot that I've never had equaled anywhere else.

The second story is about my obsession with Mt. Despair located in the heart of the North Cascades. This formidable peak doesn't welcome intruders and protects itself with dense brush, rivers, glaciers, cliff-strung valleys and more.

Nestled between is the 'Alpine Oasis'. This gallery of imagery shows off those images and places that mean the most to me, as well as the moments that stick out. These include the suffering, celebration, boot-pack, skin-track and happiness that envelope me on summits, trailheads and the places in between.

The third and final story is

about the Picket Range, an extremely rugged subrange of the North Cascades. In winter, they stand like a fortress. My week traveling through this region will never be forgotten. This book would be less without my telling of it. Included within this story is a sub-story about the Northeast Face of Mount Fury and a ski descent I made of this hair-raising route with two friends in 2003.

Lastly, I've included a short narrative about a mountain lover. She was someone that many of us treasured. Big smiles and bigger laughs enveloped a personality that positively shined. These traits and so much more defined Liz Daley. Liz, climber, mountain guide and snowboarder from Tacoma, was tragically killed in a South American avalanche. Her sudden loss has left a hole in many of us. To conclude my book, her fiancé Davide De Masi has written about her life and what it means to live like Liz.

ABOUT ME: I'm originally from Morton, Washington, and was raised on the foothills of Mount Rainier. I graduated from Western Washington University, earned my finance degree and later became a financial advisor. After 8 years working in the field, I realized I no longer wanted to be tied to an office chair, and in 2009 I quit my job. I bought a professional camera and one lens. After living off my savings for a year, I published my first images. That success grew, and today—five years later, I work as a full-time photographer.

But none of this would have happened if not for a fateful day in November 2003, the day my best friend, Ben Manfredi, drowned while kayaking. However desperately my brother and friends tried to save him, they were not able to do so. His last adventure was on the Grand Canyon of the Elwha River in Olympic National Park.

Ben was a photographer who loved writing and photography. I wanted my life to mirror his. After he passed, I took up his camera, snapped

The Hummel Family. Alpine Lakes Wilderness, Washington State.

my first images, wrote stories and kept adventuring.

Those adolescent adventures with Ben were a continuation of what began for me as a child with my brothers and parents. With them I learned to ski on the slopes of Mount Rainier before kindergarten, backpacked for weeks throughout the western United States, rode mountain bikes and rafted rivers. My life was defined by the outdoors. Or, perhaps, the outdoors didn't so much define me as much as they enhanced my childhood.

So that's my story squished into a stuff sack, carried in a heavy pack and then laid out for everyone to see. To read more, keep turning the pages. I promise, it will be worth it.

In thanks, here's a short list of those that made this dream possible.

Ben Manfredi for his enduring friendship, Josh Hummel for his undying support, Scott Hollis for his creative designing, Lowell Skoog for his inspiration, my parents, Oliver Lazenby and Norma Benson for editing, and Kyle Miller, Forest McBrian, Adam Roberts, Tim Black and Woods who were on these incredible adventures with me, all the amazing photographers I aspire to emulate such as Carl Skoog, Garrett Grove, Jordan Manley and Scott Rinckenberger, the companies that have supported me like OR, Intuition, G3, K2, Eddie Bauer, White Pass, Crystal, Alpental, REI, the magazines that share my work like Backline, Backcountry, Skiing, Mountain, Mountain Life, Coast Mountain Culture, the friends that go out there with me and let me take imagery of them even if it breaks up their run, the people like you who buy this magazine because it gets you excited and inspires you. Thanks.
I'll remember.

Sincerely,

Jason Hummel

Alpine State of Mind

Put me in cold air in high places
Wrap me in fog mixed with alien faces
Pour me into swamp
Chilled
Shiver these alp trees that huddle
From brush of wind
That drink
Such moisture filling needles that
Drip
Drip
Drip
Onto grass whose green sprouts
Spring from their seeds
And bring to life
The meadow
Of colors that cloud the alpine slopes
With rainbows of life
Whose flowers slumber all year
For the day the sun shines
And warms the rocks like bones
And awakens
The
Spring
In this place
So warm with life
Shivering in the cold

Above: My mom at Pebble Creek, Mt. Rainier National Park.

Below: My dad at Paradise, Mt. Rainier National Park.

THE AMERICAN ALPS TRAVERSE

"By forces seemingly antagonistic and destructive Nature accomplishes her beneficent designs—now a flood of fire, now a flood of ice, now a flood of water; and again in the fullness of time an outburst of organic life...." — *John Muir*

North Despair | North Cascades National Park
Washington State, USA

Bibles and books of God covered the sun-washed dash of the minivan. "I live off the grid," the middle-aged driver proudly asserted as he glanced over his shoulder and smiled back at his family.

I had been hitchhiking for hours, and this was my second ride. Sixty miles still separated me from my car.

"This is as far as I can take you," the driver said with an apologetic smile, quickly pulling over outside Marblemount, a speck of a town in northern Washington State.

"Thanks for picking me up," I gushed, waving a friendly goodbye.

My gaze followed the minivan until it melted into the sleepy shadows. Looking down, I sat and let my thoughts roll over the past 16 days.

Usually millions of neurons fire in the process of remembering. I don't visualize it so literally. To me, memory is more like a meadow, and the act of remembering is like a spring rain, followed by sunshine. Instead of flowers springing up, the greens, blues, yellows and reds of individual memories blossom.

It was no flashy color that blossomed first. It was the wet and soggy gray mid-May afternoon. At my house, in Tacoma, Washington State, I sank into my office chair. Waiting in my inbox was an unread email. The title was subtle, but that subtlety hinted at epic. It read, "Are you busy in June?"

The message included my longtime mountain companion Kyle Miller, a bipedal splitboarder. The sender was Forest McBrian, a euro-crazy but brilliant guide, whose less-than-sane ideas have always inspired in me the response of, "Yeah that could work?" Not posed as a statement, but always as a question.

Forest was fishing for partners to complete a grand traverse of Washington's North Cascades.

This is the point at which my memory flashes in another color—this time blue. It is the color in which the jovial sky envelopes our maternal sun, the color that a sprouted seed first sees when it breaks from the earth and the color of dreams becoming reality. My attempts to convince like-minded friends to join me on a similar endeavor, as Forest was suggesting, had fallen on deaf ears. It was within Northwest ski historian and pioneer Lowell Skoog's written account of his decades-long mission to ski from Mount Baker to Mount Rainier, a ~300-mile high route. In that report, he spoke of another traverse, a third of the distance, that also went across the Cascade Mountain crest. Lowell dubbed this route, traveling from Highway 20 through Glacier Peak, the "American Alps Traverse."

By 1991 Skoog and his party had made an attempt to complete the American Alps Traverse, but an uncooperative spring shut them down. In 2000, two locals took up the torch. Both Matt Firth and Bob Nielsen succeeded in reaching as far as Lyman Lake, about two-thirds of the way, but no farther.

Since that time no other known efforts have been made.

Above: Snowfield Peak, Névé Glacier. **Below:** Isolation Peak—Day 2

PART I: Highway 20 to Cascade River Road —Days 1 through 4

June 2nd: Pyramid Glacier

Red is a passionate and dangerous color. Red is the color of fear—it paints the sunrises and sunsets, and it is beginnings and endings. Yet, for Kyle Miller and me, red was the color of blood-filled mosquitoes being squashed, just like our fears. There was no Forest McBrian. He had joined the National Park Service patrol in Alaska at the last moment. The weather was questionable. One-hundred and twenty miles and 60,000 vertical feet in one of the snowiest places on Earth was hard to grasp. And we were already tired from our preparations and lack of sleep.

We arrived at the Pyramid Lake trailhead, near Diablo Lake,

smack dab in the middle of North Cascades National Park in northern Washington State, dubious of what we were getting ourselves into.

Above us, the olive-colored evergreens plugged the sky. On the road, an occasional car would hustle by. On all sides, birds voiced warnings to their friends. They know we are not like the deer; not part of the forest. Instead, we are amalgams circling the rim of civilization.

Our adventure could be broken into three parts, separated by food caches. The first is the Isolation Traverse. It was the shortest leg of our trip, expected to last four days. While short, it provided plenty of time for me to remember how to curl up in the moment and feel the heat of life as it happens.

For me, that detachment from the hubbub of city life began at the trailhead, moments before I stepped out of the car. I

Pyramid Lake trailhead

The first of many log crossings of the trip

Vine maple

joked to Kyle, "Are we really doing this?"

To which Kyle smartly retorted, "We can still go home." In a matter of speaking, we *were* at home. We both have spent more time sleeping in the mountains than in our own beds, so 'home' is quite often made where we pitch our tents and lay out our sleeping bags.

Right then, everything we owned seemed to be on our backs. I couldn't help but laugh at the thought of my monstrous load straddled on my shoulders. I often joke that I am in a relationship with my pack. We bicker, we get into arguments, and we heckle each other. In this case, I jested that she had a crush on me. In all actuality, I felt a rising urge to tell her that she is obese and barely fits inside her own skin, but I thought the better of it. I was still just feet from the car and would be spending weeks of quality time with her. Best to keep her in a good mood.

When beginning, it is best to start like one jumps into a cold lake, or in our case, a web of forest. Fully committed, we dove head-first into the leafy waves and rose as fast as we could toward the alpine zone.

Somehow a vertical mile of climbing doesn't ever go as fast as you would like, but when we burst from the greenery, our universe expanded from our feet to the horizon. To the northeast were the massive shoulders of Jack Mountain. To the northwest were the impregnable walls of the Picket Range. In between and further encompassing us were the mass of peaks that make up the formidable North Cascades. Of the 1100 glaciers in the contiguous United States, nearly 800 of them are located in the northern reaches of Washington State. It is truly a sight one has to witness and experience, especially from a summit.

Looking down at Diablo and Ross Lakes.

At a col, I looked down onto the first glacier of the trip, the Névé Glacier. Rain speckled my glasses. "So much for the great forecast," I mumbled into the gray, murky fog before agreeing with Kyle that we should set up camp there.

After dinner, I scrambled to a high perch. The clouds had cleared, and the stars shimmered. It was a perfect first night and exactly what I had come in search of. Before going to sleep, I wanted to watch the liquid blues dissolve into oily blacks. As

they did, the stars began to twinkle like the faraway city lights. The night sky inspires humility in me. That perspective, without a doubt, should humble us all.

June 3: Isolation Peak

Morning has always been coffee enough for me. I have never craved caffeine. Kyle, on the other hand, was adding four to five packets of coffee-flavored Gu to hot water. Although

Shadows stretching across the Névé Glacier.

I was happy not to be so desperate, I realized while watching Kyle consume, that he was rather pleased with his concoction.

Atop the Névé Glacier, our morning's efforts had put Kyle and me between Pyramid Peak and the Horseman. Below and ahead of us, stranded on a narrow ridge attaching the Eldorado massif to the Pyramid Massif, was the lonesome Isolation Peak. It is the namesake of the first portion of our adventure, and appropriately so. Few people have ever visited—and even fewer get to see it like we were, stretched out under puffy clouds, blanketed in snow.

Our efforts continued and brought us across rocky ridges and descended us into several small chutes, as we rushed to traverse around Isolation Peak. The few sheepish clouds in the sky were being quickly herded into our small corner of the mountains. As they neared, the sunlight came and went. We hastily made camp atop polished granite slabs. So as to dry what gear we could before the impending rain and snow, we pulled everything from our packs. Eventually, we were strung out on the rock next to our gear.

Kyle must've cracked an eyelid to see what those damn sheep-clouds were up too because not long after he cried, "Look, a rainbow!" I rolled over and looked behind me. It was too far away. I had to get closer. Jumping up, I snatched my camera, put on my boots and slid down the snowbanks that clung above cliffs. I eventually arrived at an edge. As I crept closer, I saw treed benches rolling between thousands of feet of cliffs all the way to the miniature looking forest and river below.

The view was perfect. Looking up from the valley to the mountains, I saw the rainbow again, but this time through my viewfinder. Thinking back, I wondered if, like me, Nature also remembers in colors? Perhaps a rainbow arcing through the sky is her neurons firing off? I'm just seeing her thoughts on a microscopic level. It's a beautiful idea, and who knows, perhaps the pot of gold at the end of the rainbow was never gold at all.

It was almost an hour before I tore myself away from the rainbow. By the time I returned to the tent, I was soaked through. It didn't matter.

I was juggling smiles.

I reached the tent and crawled into my sleeping bag. I couldn't sleep. I was too cold, but my chills were only skin deep.

June 4: Marble Needle

The gorilla in the room that morning was no different than any other morning. Simply: would it be sunny or not?

As I crawled from our shelter, I had my answer. Sun rays

Above the jungle.

Descending to the Névé Glacier.

Above: Wilcox Lake. **Below:** Traversing around Isolation Peak

ELDORADO PEAK

To our south, billowing clouds pile atop peaks. We
would cross this remote glacier on our third day.

danced feet away and in moments swept over me. It was like a spigot had turned on. I felt weariness, worry and exhaustion fall away. Light is so elemental and moving. I often wonder what demons humanity accepted into their homes when they replaced the wide open sky with four walls, a roof and a door.

Two hours later, my legs strained up a couloir lying between Backbone Ridge and me. More than halfway up, Kyle overtook my tracks, and he continued to lead until we reached a high point. Although I'd been there before, my last visit was encumbered in clouds. It brought a grin to life when I recalled my brother Jessy Hummel, and friends Tom Murphy and Adam Roberts on an adventure in 2011. We couldn't see a thing through the thick fog and had no idea where to go. Instead of moping, we all sat on the summit of Isolation Peak and laughed.

It wasn't the weather I had to worry about this time. Just as soon as Kyle and I transitioned onto the western flank of Backbone Ridge, the snow had transformed into isothermal mush. Now in the lead, every step I took forward brought an avalanche crashing down. A water-saturated spring snowpack is dangerous business, but we managed to find a safe enough passage until, relieved, we arrived onto colder, higher snow.

It took hours. It wasn't easy. We felt like our 'oh shit' meter had been pegged for far too long. So we stopped between Marble Needle and Morning Spire. We were wrecked. In order to get some rest as soon as possible, we dug out a camp. When we finished our platform, we pitched our tent. We were both pleased with our home for the night. Even when the bad weighs you down, good could be just around the corner.

Above camp, a rock tower perched alongside Marble Needle. On it, seemingly carved onto its stone, was the face of a wolf over 100 feet tall. *"No way!"* I scoffed, but the likeness was undeniable.

Eventually stealing my attentions, behind me I felt the sunset tuck itself

Traversing unstable snow on Backbone Ridge.

Closing in on Marble Needle.

in, under the peaks. Cool air pulsed through the tent while I prepared to sleep. At that instant, I decided to cast one final look up at the canine visage. In that moment, my heart froze. Was that its cold breath wafting into the air? Could it be howling? Of course I knew it wasn't, but the symbolism was ingrained into my subconscious.

The wolf would soon re-emerge in my dreams after sleep had devoured me. By that point, the peaks weren't peaks at all. They had mutated into wolves. I was nothing more than a man,

running. But I could leap over valleys and glaciers, and yet no matter how fast I ran, I couldn't escape them. In the end, they swallowed me whole.

June 5: Cascade River Road

Outside, dawn and wakefulness had arisen, and I could see that the mountains were still firmly rooted into the earth. That was when I grinned. I realized wolves were not chasing me. In fact, I was not the prey at all.

Above: Looking north at Backbone Ridge and Mt. Baker. **Right:** The wolf.

Above: Alpenglow and our tracks. **Right:** Images of Kyle on Backbone Ridge.

I was the wolf.

Wet boots met wet socks. That's never a happy union, but with the deed done, my crampons clanged into morning snow, each step echoing off the walls of Marble Needle Couloir on our way to the McAllister Glacier.

Rounding Eldorado Peak two hours later, we overtook the first person of the trip. Greetings passed between us followed by small talk. It was rude to do, but we sought escape as soon as we could muster goodbyes.

Kyle stopped and packed his snowboard when the snow

dipped both feet into the glacier-fed water. My screams of happy agony couldn't be quelled. Those are the moments I remember. The kind suffering rewards us.

Leaving the river, I rejoined Kyle. Pretty soon our mess of gear littered the entire northwestern corner of the Eldorado parking lot! Skirmishing with us were the orgasmic hordes of biting flies and mosquitoes. Their million eyes converged and zeroed in on our pulsing veins.

Our best escape was to cover our heads with our coats. That's how we remained until we heard the distinct rumbling

Above: Topping out on the Mcallister Glacier. **Right:** Ascending the Marble Needle Couloir.

met rock below Roush Creek Divide. I pressed on over thinly covered boulders until I felt my edges screeching from the agony of more granite than bona-fide snow. I often tend to push past the point where a wise man would give up. Sure, I'm a betting man, but I like risk, too. So when sparks flew up from my ski's edges, I was even more thrilled than when I finally slid from the boulders onto the snow and sliced one more sloppy turn.

Next to the river, thousands of knee-crunching feet lower, I found a comfortable spot atop rounded river stones. My pack dropped to the ground on the shore, while Kyle continued a few hundred yards to the trailhead. Pleased to be resting, I happily peeled my grimy socks off and hesitantly

of a car, hours later. It was our hero, James Rowe. I had only met James once, so when he offered to drop our provisions off, I felt uncomfortable asking so much from him. When he arrived and swung open his car doors, it was like an unveiling. Inside was our precious cargo, a full week's supply of food and fuel. He had come through and quickly became our new best friend, especially after he plied us with beers.

A half mile up the road Kyle, James and I found a camp. The night progressed with more drinking and talking with the added bonus of a warm fire. Memories faded into the flames. After the fire died, the coals dimmed, eventually flashing out like microscopic sunsets. It was an otherwise quiet end to a busy day.

Descending between Early Morning Spire and Marble Needle.

Above: Kyle and his horde. **Right:** Navigating the brush near Eldorado Creek.

Standing at Cache Col.

PART II: Ptarmigan Traverse to Holden Village—Days 5 through 12

June 6: Cache Col

Now my memory shifted to white—the color that is the absence of color; the color that blankets the high country; the color that fills the clouds; the color we were rising toward as we crept up Cascade River Road.

Less than two hours later, we moved from the road to snow, and continued to Cascade Pass (5,400 feet). We climbed slowly. We needed time to fall into stride and wrap our minds around the work. Once we passed Cascade Pass, I felt like I had reached that point. I charged across Mix-Up Arm, leaving Kyle far behind. As soon as we reconnected, it was his turn to leave me behind.

We rejoined at Cache Col. As we climbed over a cornice, we were surprised to meet a large group, since the only tracks we had seen so far were of two guys just ahead of us. As it turned out, this was a NOLS (National Outdoor Leadership School) group, and they had come up the rarely visited South Fork of the Cascade River.

While we rested, the NOLS leader offered us water, but we kindly turned it down. We were in for a lesson, though. It seems I didn't have a clue what a solar still was or how easy you can get water from one in the right conditions. Upon closer inspection, we figured it out. Basically, a solar still is an upside down cone carved atop the ceiling of a small snow cave. Much like a stalactite, water collects at the point and is deposited into your bottle. Brilliant! The only disadvantage was that it requires a warm, sun-saturated snowpack to work. Any unused water just flows back into the snowpack, so, "*Yes, may I have moooore please?*"

We sat. We drank. We looked around. We didn't move. The skies were teaming with clouds, and our motivation to join them wilted. We worried the next day would have bad weather. Since the only dry ground in sight was beneath our feet, we decided to find a camp and settle in.

Later that evening, we visited the NOLS group. We shared stories and laughs, and quickly became friends. Maybe just mountain friends, but that didn't matter. Our love of the outdoors was all we needed to have in common.

Above: Looking at Gunsight Peak. **Right:** The NOLS group at their camp.

Jason pondering incoming weather.

June 7: Cache Col

Much like Kyle's sleeping pad had done for every night during the past week, our hopes for a sunny day quickly deflated with morning's stolen glances out of the tent. Regardless of the soggy weather, I tried unsuccessfully to convince Kyle to pack up and go. He preferred to wait for better conditions, and I reluctantly agreed, satisfied for no other reason than the extra rest would do us good.

But rest makes me wary. There's too much time to think. To escape, I found a nice ridge to sit atop. From there I watched the fog. Over time, I tried to be like the fog—to melt over the rocks; dance above the valley and to be. Remember, being? After awhile I was present.

At dinner, my dried vegetables refused to soften, so every bite rang out with a "crack." Somehow I can get by with eating little, so I didn't worry about it. Instead my eyes feasted on the fog. They did their best to devour their way through them. My eyes are bigger than my appetite. Instead, the fog opened its mouth and gobbled me up with the night.

June 8: White Rock Lakes

Sometime in the night the fog slithered its way into the valleys. Warm air escaped. The cold took hold. The snow hardened to a sheet of ice. Not even Kyle's half-eaten and refrozen freeze-dried dinner from the night before could compete! When he attempted to consume it, the scales were nearly tipped. Was he a bear? Perhaps I'm just too picky for my own good. Kyle would outlive me for sure if we were ever stranded in the wilderness without food. He'd be eating grubs and whatever it took. I'm sure they'd be given names too. That's Mr. Miller for you, ever the dark comedian. I can see him now, "Nice to meet you, Mr. Grub…."

The morning's progress across icy slopes was completed in moments, at least for me. Kyle's snowboard edges wouldn't hold, especially on such a long toe-side traverse. He was better

Kyle Miller ascending the Le Conte Glacier.

Above: Climbing above the crux of the Chikamin Glacier. **From top right:** Laundry day; Agnes Creek; below the Chikamin; at Gunsight Notch

off cramponing. While I waited further on, lying on my back, I watched the blue sky twist itself around the sun.

On the other side of Red Ledges, with both of us riding, I traversed most of the way to the Middle Cascade Glacier. I itched to continue, but I waited. As suddenly as Kyle popped out of a nearby runnel, he was flying out of control down the slope, falling!

Jumping up, I rushed over the brow of a nearby hill just in time to see Kyle's board blowing up ice and arms flailing against the snow. He had just missed the cliffs. Some moments

later, safe but frazzled, Kyle crested the hill frightened and embarrassed. We didn't talk about his fall besides my saying something about being more careful in the future.

It wasn't until views of White Rock Lakes smiled up at us that the stars in Kyle's eyes began to sparkle again. He led the way and in less than a dozen big turns reached the shores of White Rock Lakes. Savoring the moment, I stashed my camera and followed suit. It wasn't until my last turn, after I had shuttered to a stop, that I could make out my howls ringing off the rocky escarpments.

The next few hours were spent lounging. Gear circled the food. That's when I began calculating. Could I eat my chocolate today? Should I conserve it instead? One nibble led to another. I felt like the overweight bean counter hiding in his claustrophobic cubicle. I peeled the wrapper back, and in moments, there was nothing left but chocolate dust and garbage.

June 9: Gunsight Notch

I studied my worn and crumpled hand-drawn map of a decade ago. The line curved up the Chikamin Glacier.

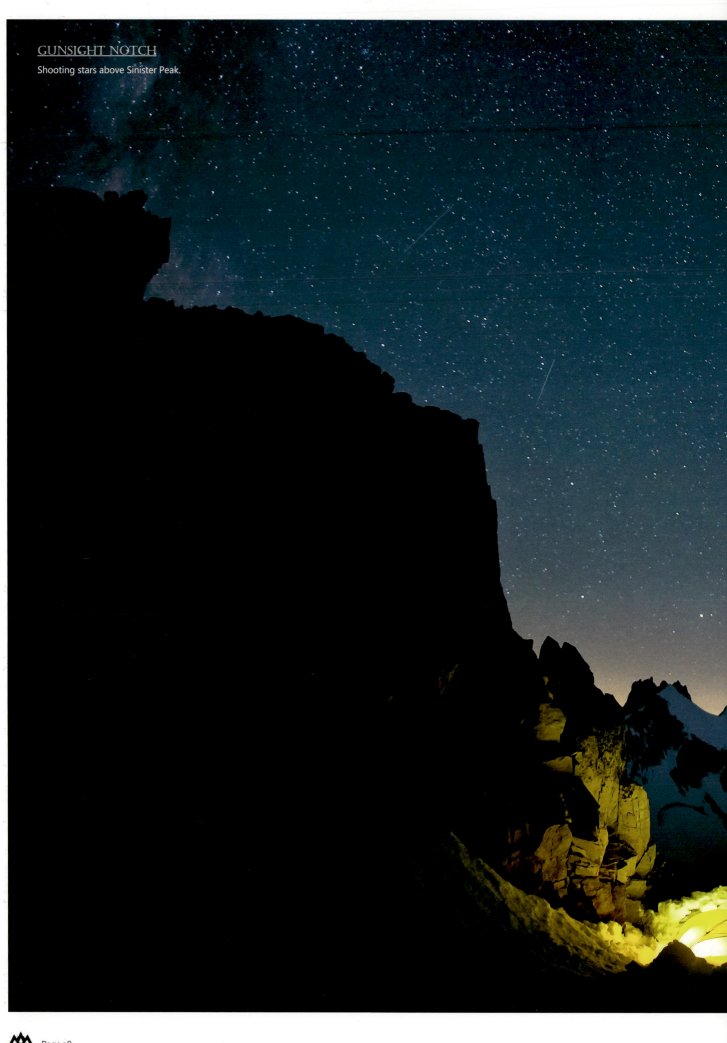

GUNSIGHT NOTCH

Shooting stars above Sinister Peak.

Looking at Agnes Mountain.

It led into one of those silent corners of the Cascades that I'd never heard of anyone traveling into—although I'm sure many had. *Privileged.* That's how I felt as I climbed beneath the towering shoulders of the immense and breath-stealing Chikamin Glacier.

Two thousand feet higher, I stood eying the cloud-shadows rolling beneath the North Face of Sinister Peak. Years before, Lowell Skoog, his brother Carl—also a photographer—my brother Josh, Jon Mauro and I became the first to ski Sinister. For one run, there was a merging of the Old Guard with the new.

It would be the last time Lowell ever skied with his brother. Together and separately, they had pioneered dozens of descents and traverses in these mountains. Sadly, a few months later, in 2005, Carl tragically fell to his death on Cerro Mercedario in Argentina.

Before his passing, back on Sinister Peak, Carl's exuberance was contagious. Like a star-struck kid, I asked all I could about imagery, and he shared what he knew to a rank amateur. What would I have asked him if I knew it'd be the last time we'd talk? Nowadays, I know better than to ask for more. Like me, his tales are told in his images; in the shades and shadows; between the curves and shoulders of mountains; within the waves and flow of streams, and glaciers; from the moods wrung from darkness and light. Bled at last, in finality, from the reds that crackle on the horizon.

The outlet falls from Bannock Lakes.

Above: Sun and shadow move across Mt. Goode. **Below:** Traversing the shore of Upper Bannock Lake.

We dug out a spot and pitched our tent at a notch below Gunsight Peak. Once I set the final anchor and seduced silty water from a crack in the cliff face, I crept up to a pinnacle to watch the sun go down. The cold and the loneliness got me thinking about mountains and how they have a way of expelling us like great lungs as they had done to Carl. When my final breath is released, I wish for it to be in a place like this, as an old man with just enough strength to make a one way trip. Not to go there to throw myself from the top, but to have my heart shake loose from my body and sink into the stone, the raw beauty too much for it.

I set my alarm for three in the morning. With my camera and tripod, I left the tent. The cold parried with my fingers. Above me the stars were so bright. I froze and pondered, "Could I reach for them?" Stretching my hands out, my palms cupped worlds like water. I felt like some great star-monster.

My life has had many memorable moments. When they happen, they surface in a magical, mystical way that my mind cocoons like a bent page from a favorite book that hides a special passage. I don't know how many hours I stayed in the open air, but outside my tent, hanging from the ridge, perched atop boulders, I sat, freezing the seconds.

June 10: Bannock Lakes

For days we had been agonizing over access to Bannock Lakes. Even as close as we were, it was hard to tell if we'd be able to arrive there without difficulty.

That morning, sunny skies led us above Blue Lake on a downward traverse. It appeared wise to cross over the ridge, so we continued over a pass onto the Garden Glacier. The

Left: Looking at the Garden Glacier on the back side of Sinister Peak. **Right:** Worn, tired and blistered feet.

grandiose views of faraway Glacier Peak and the Dakobed Range reminded me that no cityscape would ever move me as much as a mountain range.

When we arrived at Ross Pass, steep snow and patchy trees led us through steep, snow-covered boulder fields to the shores of the lowest Bannock Lake. I remembered sitting there laughing. "Did that just happen?" It was all too easy. We stretched out on the boulders with relief washing over us. I watched a nearby waterfall ricochet through a cataract from atop a massive boulder. Had we worried for nothing? Perhaps, but overcoming perceived challenges prepares you for those you least expect.

With our camp pitched between the higher Bannock Lakes, and with daylight to spare, it was time to clean up after a week marinating in my own juices. At a stream that flowed through a split in the 6-foot-high snow banks below camp, there was a clear pool beneath a waterfall. It was the perfect place for a bath.

After my body chased my toes into the frigid water, I rose back to the surface. My vision freckled with white. I leapt onto an outcrop of rock and danced around. Life rarely feels more alive than in moments like that one, when every fiber of your body is screaming, "Enough!" Makes me smile just thinking about it.

June 11: Lyman Lakes

In the early morning, at a pass high above Bannock Lakes, Kyle and I glared through spaceship flakes of snow. Some hovered but most just darted away. We were hoping to see through the fog into the valley below. Eventually we would and

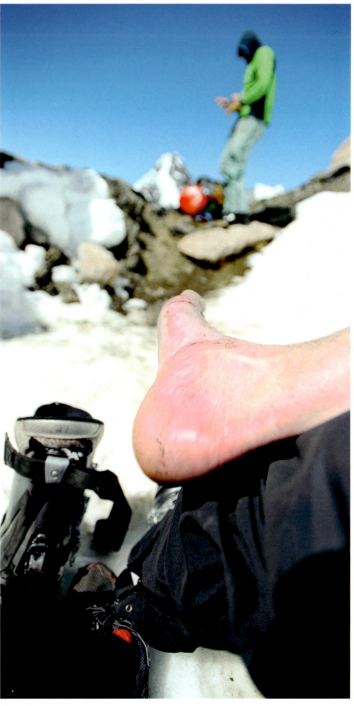

Leaving Bannock Lakes in a whiteout.

Descending to the Pacific Crest Trail.

when that small break arrived, we dove into the forest. Within moments, we had descended thousands of feet and were scrapping over the last pine-needle and tree branch riddled patches of snow until, ahead of us, we could see only dirt.

Three hours later, far below in the valley bottom next to the South Fork of Agnes Creek, near Hemlock Camp, Kyle and I weren't talking. We were at a low point. My memory was now a cauldron of blacks and reds. Blacks for the disappointment and exhaustion. Red for the anger and frustration. This wasn't just

disappointment, shrugged my pack closer and began climbing. For a while my mood mirrored the dark and gloomy weather.

At Cloudy Pass, my anger had faded, and I was exhausted. My legs teetered like the tree-giants dotting the landscape below me. My transition to downhill mode was quick. Earlier, my skins failed due to pollen and wet snow, and I had been forced to boot the entire way.

Relief lay below me, and Kyle had long since passed me by. On the shores of Lyman Lakes, I was happy. You couldn't

One of dozens of waterfalls.

the low point of the day, but of the entire trip to that point. It had begun with an earlier route disagreement. Kyle's idea had been to descend into the valley—a route I vehemently disagreed with. My plan was to stay high and return to the snow. Kyle was persistent, so I backed down, but not without insisting that his idea was foolhardy. At the river, there was a partial snowpack with heinous bushwhacking in all directions. Worst of all, it started raining. While I had been right, I didn't feel good about it. Neither of us were pleased, and we still weren't talking.

Kyle hid under a giant rock and regrouped while I turned my head toward the miles of backtracking. I shook loose the

wipe the smile off my face. Moments before, I had pushed off from the pass, allowed the grip of gravity to wind her fingers around me and felt her tug my skis downward. I didn't resist. I rode the stream bed that led down to the lake like it was a luge. At one point I flew past a waterfall, grumbling and groaning, before it burst from the snow. I swung by it at full speed, as if I were borne by the current and flung from its lip. Yes, Gravity, she is two-faced, impetuous and burdensome, but I am enamored and have always had a teenage crush on her.

Kyle and I pitched camp and scrounged up the remnants of food we had passed on every other night. This brought back

Traversing toward Cloudy Pass

The last few feet of snow before we hike.

Tent drying at Lyman Lakes

Closing in on Holden Village.

reminders of a week skiing in the Olympic Mountains. In the days leading up to that trip, Kyle had found what we called 'laundry detergent' at a grocery outlet. Basically, they were these circular-shaped, lime-flavored energy gummies with a sugar coating on top. They tasted terrible. At the time, when I asked Kyle why he ate them, he replied, "They are just calories."

That's one way of looking at what we had in front of us then, a spread of 'just calories'. I laughed and counted down the bites while huddling next to a tree, hiding from the falling snow and biting wind.

June 12: Holden Village

Above Crown Point Falls, Kyle and I hid our skis and hung our other unnecessary gear from an old snag. The views from our high vantage wiped the tiredness out of our eyes. The excitement was palpable. We were about to detour to Holden Village, where we had food and fresh supplies waiting.

As we descended into the valley, the colors and the seasons brightened. At each creek crossing I drank my fill. At each viewpoint, I feasted my eyes on the green hills, high peaks and thundering waterfalls. To pass some time, I took a swim at Heart Lake while waiting for Kyle. Neither of us were in a hurry. Our hunger was forgotten. Maybe the mind requires more nourishment than the flesh?

Either way, the hike soothed me. Weariness blew off me like the leaves from the vine maples that leaned over the trail.

Four hours passed. We slipped from the meadows into the forest and from the forest into Holden Village. It would be my fourth time there in three years. Prior to the 1960s, the town was a home for miners who worked one of the biggest copper mines in the nation. In the 50 years since, it has existed as an idyllic hamlet, owned and operated by the Lutheran Church as a retreat. This had changed little over the decades, until recently. In 2009, hundreds of workers were sent in to stabilize tailings and contain toxins from entering nearby Railroad Creek. The old mine is a superfund site and for good reason. Railroad creek eventually flows into Lake Chelan, the 26th deepest freshwater lake in the world. While troublesome to see the changes, they are for the best in the long term.

Bringing my eyes back down from the mine above, I imagined what other people saw when looking at Kyle and me. We didn't have street clothes, just ski attire. We carried the mountains in our skin and bones. The valleys furrowed our faces. The summits shone in our eyes. We most certainly were an unsightly lot.

Our first stop was the cafeteria, in the main lodge. Once inside, our hunger-crazed eyes feasted on the plethora of meats, cheeses, pies and more. I'd never been so famished as I was then. Living off a diet that rarely exceeded 1,500 calories a day had taken its toll. Even though Kyle had carried twice the calories, what we burned per day per person far exceeded what we had combined.

You could imagine my sadness, when, halfway through a sandwich I realized something was wrong. My least favorite food is mustard, and I didn't need to look to know the bread was slathered in that vile, yellow poison. My brothers and I often joke that mustard is 'Hummel Birth Control'. All a girl has to do is eat mustard, and we will have nothing to do with her for sometime after.

A liter of water, then a refill, some gurgling, and I was recovered, at least physically. Kyle laughed at me as he consumed the rest of my sandwich, along with his.

On the far wall was the daily forecast, pegged among the other community fliers. I swept over to it, scared. As I read down the page, my hands stopped shaking. It wasn't great, but it wasn't terrible either. "The bad news," I told Kyle as he polished off the last bite of my sandwich, "we have to leave in the morning. The good news, I think we may just be able to pull this off!"

Well past darkness, we sauntered out of town and pitched camp. I felt like I'd won the lotto, even as I kicked the ants from my bed. Struggle and effort had brought us here, but nothing had gotten us farther than luck. No June I could recall had ever been as forgiving as this one.

Consulting the map.

Closing in on food and shelter.

Please sir, I want some more!

Above: Traversing the summit ridge of Fortress Mountain with Glacier Peak in the distance. **Below:** Kyle's expression is worth a million words.

PART III: Holden Village to the White Chuck River—Days 12 through 16

June 13: Upper Lyman Lake

Holden is an oasis surrounded by wilderness. We returned to town that morning to pick up our resupply. Now we were rounding the first bend outside town, leaving for good. I sighed and dug my toes into the dirt, forcing myself to leave the homely comforts behind.

The miles back to Lyman Lakes melted away like the countless meadows. Hardly a word passed between us until we were reacquainted with our gear stashed the day before above Crown Point Falls.

Another hour later, we found respite from blowing snow in a tuft of trees near the uppermost Lyman Lake. I laid against a cold tree again. I ate a plain meal. I made faces at the fog, and it made faces back.

And so went the evening.

June 14: Fortress Mountain

I arose to fog the next morning. It scraped down the faces, hung on the sleepy shoulders and sank into the valley. The same valley I stood in looking at the blue-eyed waters of Lyman Lake.

Halfway up Chiwawa Mountain, I stopped. The sky was staring at me. Light and shadow shot through clouds, leaving sapphire holes behind. Turning my head to the climb above, I continued and met Kyle at a narrow ridge. By then, we had been submerged. The fog had tied its shoelaces.

We couldn't outrace the white nothingness.

Atop Chiwawa Mountain, I kicked snow from my crampons onto the melted-out rocks. Boot packing up the remaining 500 feet from the ridge was difficult. Thinking about it made me grimace. While I love to suffer, it is only because I eventually overcome. There were a few moments when struggling up that I wanted to throw my hands up in the air. These conditions were ridiculous. The breakable crust was just strong enough to hold my body weight for a step or two … or five? There was

FORTRESS MOUNTAIN
A brocken spectre and Kyle rising above the fog.

FORTRESS MOUNTAIN, SOUTHWEST FACE
Dropping in with Buck Mountain looking on in the distance.

no predicting your eventual collapse. Without warning, we'd be postholing. Kyle and I took turns. Those grimaces evolved; they became smiles.

We were winning.

Leaving the summit, through the smoky skies, I rained snow down the mountain in search of a way through. Was my map lying? Was I lying to myself? Like a sphincter, the cliffs closed in. "Shit," I thought. I really didn't want to climb back out. So I kept going—and I won, again. The rocks vanished, and all I could see were fields of white snow. I beckoned Kyle down by yelling as loud as I could.

We descended and stopped, struck like a nail between Fortress and Chiwawa Mountains. My eyes strained. I searched the fog. I didn't know where to go from there. With only bad options, I chose to take the high route over the summit of Fortress Mountain. It was the most risky of the options, but I was convinced it would go. Kyle was doubtful, and rightfully so, but I didn't need to remind him of our adventures in Agnes Creek and our descent into that misbegotten hag of a valley to win this argument. This was mine. Fortress Mountain and I had history.

Everything Kyle had feared was staring him in the face a short time later. I was only getting more determined. I laughed as I reached up for a rocky handhold. Instead of stone, I found a rappel sling to hang from. Looking down I saw Kyle. He looked up at me and groaned, "How does it look?"

Was it more cruel to lie or to tell the truth? I leaned to the side of optimism; I lied. "It looks way better," I threw down like a bomb. I lit the fuse. "If we can traverse this rock slope, I think we can get there," I added. Kyle's eyes erupted in fire, but he said nothing. He was as determined as I was.

To either side of us were long-faced cliffs, looking sad and dejected. I felt their hunger and teeth. They were starving. I fed them scraps of stone as I grappled with my crampons. I then crossed ice-layered boulders, pivoted across smooth granite and finally leapt lightly to the snow, and only then did I feel success creeping in for a kiss. Ten dangerous steps on a porous 60-degree snow slope and I was onto rock again. A few vertical moves and I was there. The clouds melted away, the peaks turned to look at me, and the sun put her lips to mine. This was among the happiest moments of my life.

I watched my shadow dance within a Brocken Spectre, a natural phenomenon I've only seen three other times. How could it get any better? If it could, I didn't know how. I couldn't take my eyes off the specter and its kaleidoscope of colors. They circled as if submerged in oily water.

Only when Kyle squeezed by me did I join him in our march along the narrow ridge. First to the summit, Kyle stopped and raised his hands. He let escape the loudest yell I'd ever heard him make. Was he roaring a challenge at Glacier Peak? It was

Descending into the fog.

Warming up next to a cozy fire.

our last great obstacle. I like to think he was. I like to think it heard him.

On the descent, I was ready to meet a demon. Remember, Fortress Mountain and I had history. It goes back to 2008. Mere feet from the summit, an avalanche swept me up and carried me a thousand feet down the steep, cliff-riddled flanks. I was lucky to survive.

This time, I fully expected that old demon to raise hell. It didn't. There was nothing. No fear in my head. No shaking in my bones. Just joy as I raced down the entire route, stopping only twice for pictures.

We made camp near the base of Fortress Mountain after skiing to the tail end of the snow. We were happy to be on dry ground. The Buck Creek Pass trail was a few hundred feet away. We were lucky. We had found an established camp. After our routines, we made a fire. It wasn't long before I felt the heat sink into my bones. I didn't want to head back to the tent. Somehow I felt this day had to end with an exclamation mark. (Exclamation)!

June 15th: Tenpeak Mountain

When I was a kid I completed a 16-day hike around Glacier Peak. I was joined by my parents and two brothers. There were a handful of places I remembered from that adventure—one was Buck Creek Pass and the surrounding flower fields; another was High Pass.

When I stood at High Pass, looking down into Triad Lake, I smiled. I smile a lot, and moreso when memories from past and present collide. They enrich my experiences. I am fascinated by the evolving nature of a place; the change of seasons; the march of years.

Kyle and I turned on the afterburners once we reached the Napeequa Valley. Kyle had been there just a few months earlier. He was familiar with where to go, so we dug deep and pushed down the throttle. At Tenpeak, we pitched our tent near where Kyle and I had camped when we completed the Dakobed Traverse in 2010. Snaking down to camp was the couloir I had skied solo. I ached to do so again. But so close to the end, I knew we simply couldn't afford the time.

After so much effort, our success hung in the balance. "Just one more day," I whispered. The wind fluttered the tent, as if to answer my question. I didn't hear what it had to say, but I hoped it was good.

June 16th: White Chuck River

When the tent flap opened, sunlight swept in. It bashed through the doors like a gunslinger into a saloon.

Climbing through glacier lilies in the Napeequa Valley.

Above: Closing in on High Pass. **Below:** Shooting stars beneath Tenpeak.

On the shores of the Honeycomb Glacier and terminal lake, we stopped although we didn't need to. We certainly could've just kept on going, but beautiful places deserve a handshake and small talk at the very least. It would be rude to just drink, eat and leave.

Atop the Honeycomb Glacier, we stood above the Suiattle Glacier. Kyle went low, and I traversed high. We both met on the ridge above the Cool Glacier and took another break, but it was short-lived. Up ahead was our goal, the one we had been focused on all this time—Glacier Peak.

And we were impatient. But it wasn't just us, so was the weather.

Two hundred feet before the summit, I was on my knees.

Kyle was right behind me. We had been going so fast; too fast. My legs threatened to buckle. Can you believe that? Weeks of touring—I was as strong as I've ever been. While mentally I could push on, physically I was at my limit. I had nothing left. Then I heard the buzzing. I know that sound. Above me the sky had a dark expression. I saw lightning dancing on the peaks in the distance. The buzzing? It was the electricity in the air crackling on my ski edges!

Thunder fell onto my ears, shook my soul and you know what, I was excited. It was like fireworks. It was bombs bursting. It was a celebration. Yeah, there was no one else but us, just mountain peaks leaning in.

Then, like that, we were on the summit. Never had I put so

Above: Watching storm clouds on the Cool Glacier. **Right:** Descending the Sitkum Glacier.

Resting at Honeycomb Lake.

Colorful bands of rock on the Honeycomb Glacier.

much physical effort into completing a singular goal in my life. I fell to my knees again. I took in those feelings of success. I swam back through the memories: the colors; the blue sky; the blue-eyed lakes reflecting back; the white clouds; the white snow; the yellow sun; the yellow meadows of glacier lilies; the black sky poked through with starlight; the rainbows; the spectrum of memory; the melting pot.

The now.

The wind stopped. The snow petered out. Then the sunlight slipped out between the fleshy folds of dark thunderheads. I took my camera out. I took a picture of Kyle holding his board in the air. I took a picture of both of us.

Then we left.

I wondered if the mountains even noticed our passing.

I looked at our exit route down the Sitkum Glacier. For Kyle and me, it was the obvious route. The White Chuck Trail had long been wiped out for most of a decade now. It was a horrible exit. *Perfect*, we thought. That's the standard we wanted to set. Why make it easy? Plus, it was logical to go up and over the summit, not to backtrack.

My last time on the Sitkum Glacier was in 2001. The road was snowed in. I had to graduate from college the day after the climb. My whole family was coming. Somehow my friend Ben Manfredi convinced my twin brother Josh and me to make a one-day push and ski descent of the Sitkum Glacier. Nearly 30 miles with the added road. It was brutal.

Crossing a creek on our way to the Suiattle River.

We made it, though. The worst part was the drive home. I remember yelling at my brother, exclaiming, "There's a barn in the center of the road!" It was the first time I ever hallucinated. Somehow I thought the barn had ripped loose from the slope above the highway and crashed down to the pavement. My brother wiped his tiredness from his eyes and drove. I can't blame him. We both arrived at our graduation in the morning, a little worse for wear.

In our escape down the Sitkum Glacier, we enjoyed over 5,000 feet of descent. At Glacier Meadows, Kyle and I negotiated steep forest, waterfalls and cliffs and didn't come upon any trail until we arrived at the valley bottom. Somewhere in-between it had begun to rain.

With tired feet, sore knees and crumpled motivations, we took a poorly maintained trail down to the White Chuck River and pitched camp. Next to a log, we lit a fire. The warmth of the flames pulled the cold from our bones and re-energized us. We shared stories and laughed about the highs and lows.

June 17th: White Chuck River

The rain had shaken itself out of the clouds by morning. Today I feared would be interesting. On a sign the day before,

we had seen scratched into the wood, "Trail does not exist."

"How bad can it be?" Kyle and I joked. "It's a trail, and we haven't been on one of those in days."

Well, the simple answer was "Bad!" At one point, I wondered if it would have been better to beeline from Glacier Peak to the nearest town, but no, that wouldn't have been good. Why rob myself of this adventure?

Steep hillsides had torn away into the river. The trail had crossed through these hillsides. It remained clinging, here and there, between mudslides. Otherwise, it was gone. I can't tell you how many times we were nearly crushed by a boulder or ripped the brush loose from the hillside, only to be spared by another boulder or more brush.

The cuts and bruises added up.

After hours, we left the river and its torments behind. New ones presented themselves. We crawled under, over, up and around giant old-growth and eventually came to the trailhead, where the road met us. Even that was anticlimactic. The road was overgrown with grass. Even trees pushed up through the gravel. Ahead was 8 more miles. We hiked past more washouts and fallen trees.

We arrived at the gate. On the other side, Kyle and I dropped our packs. The weight slid from our shoulders, the weight of weeks of effort. The bugs swarmed, but we didn't care.

My car was still at the Pyramid Lake trailhead, over 100 miles away. I volunteered to run a further 10 miles out to the highway where there'd be a chance of flagging down a passing car. My plan was to drive back, once I arrived at my car, and pick up Kyle. Until then, he would wait for me.

I took only a coat, flashlight, water and camera. I didn't think I could run. My legs were too tired, weren't they? I picked up my feet and began to jog. The wind, the sounds of the river, the rustle of leaves—these sounds all reverberated in my head. Somewhere between Darrington and Kyle, I stopped. I didn't want to finish. I didn't want to go forward or backward. I wanted to stay, but I couldn't.

Hours later, I was stuck in the darkness along Highway 20 after the minivan with the 'Bibles and books of God' had pulled away. It appeared my luck had faded. I tried to pace, but I didn't have the energy anymore. My feet were too tired.

Above: Searching for the trail. **Below left:** Trail? **Below right:** "Could not find; trail does not exist."—Etched advice from those who preceded us.

Sitting on the pavement, I reached down and peeled a chunk off the sole off my shoe. I grinned. Would a chunk of me come off if I tried? The thought scared me back to paying attention to the passing cars. No more passed as the hours ticked by.

Just when all hope evaporated, a mangled car pulled up, a dog shoved his face out the window, and an old man hollered, "Where are you going?".

"I'm heading over the pass," I said, still optimistic that someone would be going over it so late in the day.

"I'm heading that way, jump in!" he offered as he reached over and opened the door. "It will be nice to have company."

After introductions, I noticed a pair of skis in the back of his car. They were from the 70s, or perhaps the early 80s. I mentioned them, and he groaned, "I tried to get a job at a ski area this year. I used to be a part of the ski patrol down south, decades ago." I couldn't imagine him skiing, let alone joining the patrol in the shape he appeared in then. My opinion changed when he added, "I live in my car now; not sure where I'll be going." To me he hung his dreams, however ill-conceived, on those skis, something a younger man would do, and we'd celebrate him for doing.

As we pulled up to my car, I shook the old man's hand and told him how much I appreciated him stopping for me. And as he drove away, I shouted, "Best of luck!" while his hand waved back at me from his window. When his lights vanished, there was only quiet and me left in his wake.

Looking up into the dark forest into where we began our journey 16 days before, I shuddered. There was no color at all, just darkness, but not so for my memories. They were a vibrant meadow stretching in all directions, full of the blues, greens, yellows and reds, and every other color I had remembered. When I looked back down at the black pavement, I closed my eyes. In my head, the sun was setting, but I knew that a new day would rise. Any adventurer knows that life is not measured in weeks, months or even years, but in the adventures realized.

With that final thought, I grappled with the keys and cranked the ignition, returning down Highway 20, back into civilization, on to my next adventure. ◭

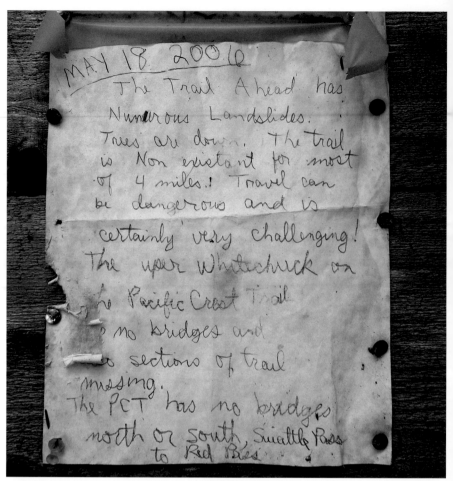

Trailhead advice that remains relevant all these years later.

One of more than a hundred logs separating us from the end.

Above: Kyle forging a new trail on the White Chuck River. **Below:** Where's the welcoming party?

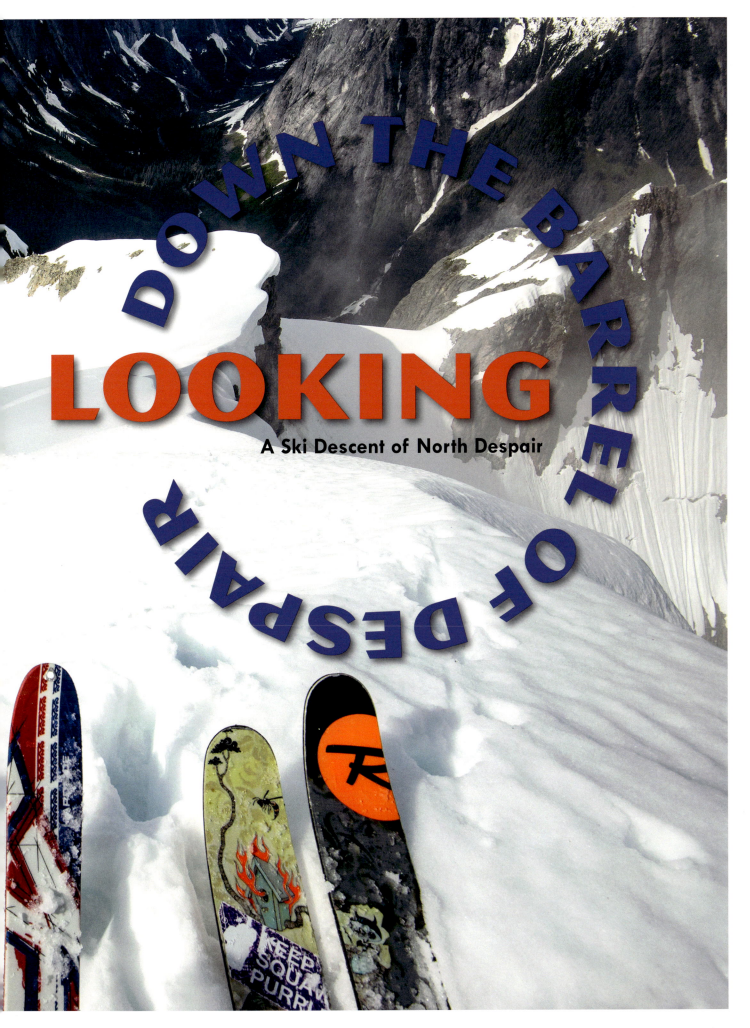

LOOKING DOWN THE BARREL OF DESPAIR

A Ski Descent of North Despair

The '60s.

The '70s.

The '80s.

North Despair | North Cascades National Park | Washington State, USA

Mountains are my church. They teach me, but they don't keep me. While I will tempt my fate, I usually know better than to overstay my welcome.

Going back a decade, that sentiment holds as true as ever. Three close friends and I listened to our logical minds and ran from Washington State's Southern Pickets in the wake of a toxic spring snowpack and belching thunderheads.

When our hurry slowed, we sulked. It was then my eye caught its first views of North Despair and her snowy arête. So perfect—her long nose of snow—that my skis pointed toward her like the arrow of a compass.

Then I forgot about her.

Only when my eyes perused my worn maps at home was the spark rekindled. So many memories are written in those tight contour lines that they are like strings playing a tune that hums the story of my life.

But North Despair was no bright-eyed maiden or damsel in distress. She was a lady of the court and had left me with quite the impression. Her wiles had transgressed the decade; I was enamored and no matter what it took, I would set off to visit her.

June 2nd: Baker Lake

On June 2nd, 2014, I parked at the trailhead for Baker Lake on the edge of North Cascades National Park, elevation 660 feet. When I stepped out of the car, lush shades of green engulfed me. A wind wafted between tree trunks and rolled over the surrounding foliage like ocean waves.

After an hour, my gear was sorted and packed, and I chased my ski partners, who were already on their way. Like me, they wanted to get the hard part done. Any progress they hoped to gain was slowed by their week of supplies; the weight of it all folded them over like accordions and their groaned exclamations were poor musicians.

On the way in, I barely saw Adam Roberts and Tim Black, two friends I knew before the trip. Beyond them and out of sight was the enigma, Woods. If he had a first name, I never heard it, and would guess that few have.

Our group was a generational melting pot. The four of us were born in different decades. Woods the '60s, I was from the '70s, Adam the '80s, and the youngster, Tim, the '90s.

We never lacked conversation, at least not the kind appropriately matured for the consumption of most 12 year olds. These mannerisms, it appeared, are transgenerational.

The '90s.

Scott Croll on Pioneer Ridge, June 1989. *Photo by John Dittli.*

Near Blum Creek, water hummed in the distance. No more than a mile from the trailhead, we turned left into the forest.

From this creek we forged our own path. There was no longer a manicured trail to follow. Our path from here would be where we made it. While I have been here, the others hadn't. I warned them of its joys.

I tallied up the previous times I'd gone this way; it was four. A knowing smile curled my lips. None of them went well. The worst was in 2005, with Sky Sjue and my twin brother, Josh Hummel. The trouble came after skiing the Northwest Face of Mount Blum in a whiteout and whirling snowstorm in the middle of February.

During that long ago exodus to Baker Lake, two of three flashlights died. Cold, wet and lost, we struggled off route through rain that was half as much snow as water and over terrain that was half as much cliff as fallen trees. When we arrived at the bottom, I kissed the dirt of the Baker Lake trail, jokingly. But it was no laughing matter. It isn't a particularly dangerous place to be, especially on route. My trouble has usually come because I've tried to descend in the dark and in a hurry.

That misbegotten adventure, coupled with three more to the Mount Blum region, encompasses my experience southwest of Mount Despair. Another five adventures into the Picket Range make up my experience northeast of Mount Despair.

Sandwiched by these previous adventures, the meat of the region has remained unknown to me. I'm not alone. Few people have visited.

The first party on skis came in 1989. It consisted of North Cascade National Park rangers John Dittli and Scott Croll. In their pioneering adventure, they crossed from Bacon Peak through the Picket Range.

After they crossed Mystery Ridge, Ditti wrote in his journal, "... the place had an ominous feel to it; partly due to the physical characteristics, but mostly due to perception; it was late in a long day, shady and cold. I looked at Scott and asked, 'If you think your time is up we probably shouldn't go.' We went."

In completing this traverse, Dittli and Croll did what I consider one of the crowning achievements of Cascade traverses.

Only two years later, Cliff Leight and Dana Hagin retraced Dittli and Croll's path from Bacon Peak and Mystery Ridge. Beyond there, they diverged and traversed the shoulders of North Despair and Mount Triumph and exited near Highway 20, Washington's northernmost transmountain highway.

Since these skiers, no others are known to have returned, and North Despair had yet to be skied. This combines two of my favorite pastimes: retracing ski tracks and making new ones.

Back on the hills that rise above Baker Lake, I grasped the huckleberry bushes that clung 2,000 feet above the valley floor. Waves of sweltering, muggy air rung me out like a rag; the sweat on my brow mixed with spider webs, dirt and fir needles. When I wiped this jungle soup away, I merely succeeded in stirring more into the mix.

My wandering thoughts eventually focused on the melody of leaves, logs, thorns, fallen trees, vine maple and marshes that clawed at me in my passing. All of it formed a great, green wall. This approach is not alone in that regard. Many peaks in the Cascades have similar armor. They shield themselves from the casual interloper. This reason is among the greatest of those that fan my love for the Cascade Mountains. You must earn their approval and admittance, and the green wall is the accountant and the tax man wrapped into one.

I unclipped my skis from my pack and snapped them onto my feet three hours later. The weight off my shoulders was a relief after nearly a vertical mile of jungle-bashing up a hillside. I've heard it said, "One pound on your feet is equal to five pounds on your back." That may be true in some sports, but not skiing. According to this calculation, my 20 pounds of ski gear was equal to a 100 pounds on my back. This is tomfoolery. I traded my skis from my back to my feet in a second.

When I rose above the trees, the sun and her 93-million-mile smile blinded me. Residual daylight melted into sunset. It boiled orange with thunderheads and sun rays, and swallowed us as we pitched camp at 5,800 feet on a narrow ridge. From that vantage, we enjoyed views in all directions.

Woods returns to his natural environment.

Adam Roberts crossing the Baker River.

As night spread over us, the clouds retreated to wherever they had come from. In their wake, stars freckled the heavens overhead. They seemed to make passes at all of us, but none could hold our eyes for long. Flashier, brighter versions filled the celestial ceiling, dancing far better than our two left feet could ever manage to match.

Instead of sleep, Adam decided it was time to ski. Perhaps he thought he could go toe to toe with the stars? Either way, these odd hours added to the allure and excitement. I took up my camera instead of snapping on my skis. I craved to join, but only would an hour later after I crawled into bed and dreamed of it.

June 3rd: Berdeen Lake

Restful sleep numbed the wounds of the previous day. Breakfast, we decided, would be enjoyed 800 feet lower on the shores of Blum Lakes.

After the ski, Adam volunteered to downclimb the upper Blum Lake's snow bank for water. Conveniently there was a snow-free rock a few feet from the snow bank on the lake's shore to jump on top of. Although, when he jumped, he failed to reach it. The snow bank collapsed, and he fell into the cold lake water. We howled in laughter while Adam stood shin deep, and growled in disgust. Wet boots are about the worst kind of torture you could ask for.

By chance my camera recorded the moment Adam fell

in. The laughter resumed for a second time, just as loud as the first as I replayed his flop. The only difference was the fresh mountain water we had in hand. The laughter had given me a terrible thirst. Grinning, I thought of raising my bottle and saying, "Adam, more water please?"

With breakfast done, my partners gathered their gear and skied across the frozen half of Blum Lake. For a few moments, I lingered behind. I focused on the unfrozen lake waters that make up the closer half of the lake. They are deep green, brushed with shades of blue. While the surface reflected the mountain cliffs above, I wondered if from somewhere deep below a consciousness looked up at me and wondered the same thing as I did. "Is there anyone there? If so, what is he thinking?"

Of course I had no answer, so I skied away.

Eventually I caught up. In front of me, Woods cut an elegant skin track for more than two miles across the Hagan Glacier. Few splitboarders can manage such a feat; Woods is one of them.

As I continued trekking, I often paused and smiled wildly. You must understand the moment. The temperatures weren't cold like in winter. They bathed me, as if I were in a lukewarm bath. The snow wasn't powder, but a few inches of corn snow, thawed by the sun. Some folks believe winter is what skiing is all about. There's a secret though, that a few of us take for granted. Come spring it is t-shirts, sunscreen, shades and, most importantly, relatively safe skiing and travel. The difference is the chairlifts are closed, and you have to work for it. That's no problem for us. It's what we crave.

Lunch was enjoyed on a flat bench. I felt like I was a small child trying to sit in an adult's chair; my face just peeking over to see everyone's faces. Across the table was Mounts Baker and Shuksan, both adoring mothers who would admonish us for our barbaric eating habits.

Over a narrow pass, at 6,650 feet, soft algae-layered snow led us down into a tightly guarded valley. Standing overhead, a handful of peaks stood shoulder to shoulder. At the base, hidden between them, are two lakes. Frozen, with their glistening waters hidden, there was an intimacy this time of year offered that summer couldn't. Dressed in white snow, we could only imagine them stripped down, surrounded by green fields and pockets of spring flowers. The attire made her all the more sexy. It was a woman in a suggestive dress, poised and graceful.

It wasn't until 1922 that Ernest Kobelt and Jim Jaeger laid eyes on Berdeen Lakes, the first known to have done so. They didn't name the lakes, though. That story goes back even further. According to local pioneer John Roper, it traces back to Glee Davis, who emigrated to the Skagit Valley in the early 1900s. Glee, it turned out, named present day's Pyramid Peak after a childhood friend, named Bernadine. A local forest manager at the time removed that name and placed the incorrectly spelled name of 'Berdeen' to the body of water between Mount Hagan and Mystery Ridge.

Just beyond shore, on lower Berdeen Lake, we sighted a small island. Since there were exposed rocks that we could rest on, we aimed for it and placed our camp nearby.

With much daylight to spare, the snow slopes surrounding our camp soon bore individual signatures, those arcs and sweeps of turns particular to

Above: Woods leaves the trail for good. **Below:** The group reaches solid snowpack.

Adam breaking free of the forest.

Sun rays on Mt. Baker.

Above: Tim, the moon, Mt. Baker and dinner. **Below:** Adam Roberts skiing beneath stars.

Adam working his way toward Mt. Hagan.

the skier. It wasn't until the last rays of light flashed out. Not until after the orange and red blistered the thready filaments of wind-whipped clouds over Mount Hagen that we returned to camp. Once there, completely exhausted, our feet dangled from cliffs and smiles from faces.

June 4th: North Despair

Mornings are cold, like castles of medieval days. Although, unlike those bygone gentry that filled them, we'd have no fire to warm us. Instead, a cold wind curled under our skin and raked her fingers through our hair.

I left the tent and shouldered my pack. The snow crackled with each step. Unlike the previous two days, we would not be continuing our traverse. Instead, we would be making a detour with only day packs. This was the day we'd point our skis toward my ultimate goal, North Despair.

At a pass a mere 500 feet above camp, Woods, our sole splitboarder, decided to return the way he had come. Two things concerned him—the icy snow and slowing us down. He'd have to boot every step of the way while we quickly and efficiently scooted across the slopes on our narrower skis.

From the pass, we bidded Woods best of luck. He returned the sentiment and that was the last we saw of him before he melted into the shadowed slopes behind us.

Eventual fog nipped at our ankles and chewed at our

confidence. The way ahead was hidden by the thick haze. The glimpsed views offered little relief. Holding onto the unknown and the fear, I smiled widely. This is what I seek out. It is what I crave. If I knew the way, all her secrets, then it would be sport, not adventure.

My fascination couldn't have been more stoked or my mind more on fire. It roared into an inferno as I climbed to the top of Full Pack Peak and gazed eastward. The fog had sunken into the valleys. The sky was blue as an alpine lake. My view beyond was unhindered. Gazing freely toward my mountain, not that any mountain could ever be mine, I wondered, "did Mount Despair recognize me?" I would like to think that she did.

Atop Full Pack Peak, now above the fog, I gathered in my placement among these towers of earth. As I rotated 360 degrees, I further appreciated these mountains layered upon mountains. No cities or roads anywhere to be seen, just layer upon layer of wilderness. Magical. Mystical. Momentous. Mine.

Mystery Ridge, as the name suggests, has underlying mysteries to be sleuthed out. The greatest, when it concerned us, was to find a way from Mystery Ridge to the base of the West Face of North Despair. It was the crux.

Our route looked better than expected. We crept by a massive cornice and then descended in a long, slanting

Above: Nearing the top of the Hagan Glacier. **Below:** Getting a good look at the surrounding scenery.

BLUM LAKES

Gazing into the Mountain-eye.

Above: Dawn at Berdeen Lake. **From top:** Sun salutation; Tim packing; Arriving at Berdeen Lake; Descending from Mystery Ridge.

traverse to a point where we climbed a hundred feet to a break in a ridge. It seemingly offered a route from the hanging valleys, whose surrounding cliffs hung below us, to the snowfields below. With each progressive turn, questions turned to certainties then back to questions.

I find sheltered in wilderness corners places where shadows grow like wheat in a field. They are treacherous places. They are foreboding. This was such a place. Cliffs towered and hung overhead. Broken snow gripped onto bedrock that threatened to lay waste to everything below if so much as a breath of an excuse passed its way. Those bergs of snow only highlighted the need to hurry. We didn't linger. We didn't dare pause. I've always felt, however unlikely, that shadows have souls in places such as this.

Once we skied free from the shadows, we were all smiles and swagger as we arrived onto easier slopes. The way ahead was opened. The key fit. The door unlocked. We skinned across gentle slopes and felt success within our grasp.

Soon, my figure outlined the North Ridge of the North Peak of Mount Despair. It silhouetted the line I saw from Mount Degenhardt a decade ago. The memory forced a grin onto my face. The moment couldn't be more perfect. The wind silenced. The sun posed. I half expected to hear echoes of rocks falling or a hawk caw-cawing from miles away. Instead our only company was heartbeat and breath.

Stopping near the top, my eyes scoured the terrain; I was aghast. The place was a medieval fortress, as I knew all too

MYSTERY RIDGE

Fog enveloping Adam and Tim.

FULL PACK PEAK

A wall of clouds crashes into Mystery Ridge.

Adam descending toward North Despair.

Booting the north ridge of North Despair.

well. But, even so, the broken rock and leaning towers, ancient weather-worn trees, the uncultivated valleys and the much guarded secrets welled up in me, a sense of awe I couldn't tame.

I screamed as loud as I could from the top of North Despair. Only a few instances I recalled have ever been its equal. It was a crack in my soul. It was my happiness untethered from my body.

This, sir/madam, is why I adventure!

That thrill of mine, it is measured in decibels (!!!).

Our hurry increased. Dusk was fast approaching. We rushed back to the top of Mystery Ridge. By then, I was like a stretched rubber band. I wouldn't stop being pulled until I was at camp resting.

As the sun crossed the horizon, the snow froze and shadows grew near the top of Full Pack Peak. One second it was soft, spring corn and then, moments later, rock-hard

Behind Tim, far below, is the guts of the Picket Range.

Slithering clouds stole our sun and blue sky. Waiting for it to clear, I laid on the summit rocks. Nearby the others found their own cubby of stones. The weather eventually broke. It was all too soon.

We lined our skis on the summit, staring down into the barrel of Despair.

I pushed off first, then Adam and Tim. There was no stopping us now. We skied all the way down. Like that, three days of effort were compressed into seconds. Was it worth it? Sure. My evidence is this: Remember my scream? Yes, those screams again. It's my answer to you.

ice. From my vantage, blood-red clouds seared the sky over Mount Shuksan. They attracted me. At first the view was mesmerizing. That quickly changed as I edged closer to a cornice and searched for a better angle to photograph it. Suddenly, I stopped. I put my camera away. I knew that it was unwise to draw closer to the edge, like a fly to the flame, but risk is high while in reverence. I still looked, though, but instead just allowed my eyes to record the moment. That was best, to simply allow my vision to be harnessed, and dragged across the sky.

Fourteen hours since we had left, we strolled into camp.

Tim Black peering down from the summit of North Despair.

The descent.

Wispy clouds float over Mystery Ridge.

Our route from Mystery Ridge follows the broken snow.

A light blinked on, and Woods rolled out of bed.

Sitting on our island's ledges, we shared highlights. At the same time, Adam began peeling the skin from a blister on the heel of his foot. We all cringed, laughed and then slipped into bed, exhausted, but contended. A day lived to its fullest, no doubt, is best capped with thrill-glinted eyes closed upon star-glinted heavens.

June 5th: Mount Hagen

Morning rose sunny and beautiful. Naps were interrupted by the perfect weather. It was a shame, really. We could've slept all day. Our biggest trouble was how to shield the sun from our eyes. A shirt, sleeping bag or arm worked for awhile, but eventually it wasn't enough.

It was time to go.

Our tracks slithered across the flat expanse of Berdeen Lake, leaving camp behind like a newly made friend you promised to visit, but knew you'd never see again.

At the outlet, I inched toward a narrow chasm in search of a way beyond the cliff bands that blocked forward progress. The closer I came, the more the water's power strummed the chords of air and fear. Emboldened, I held onto gnarled

View of Mt. Triumph from Mystery Ridge.

trees, leaned over and stared into the maw. It fixated me like a dragon spitting fire. You can't tear your eyes away from that no matter how hard you try!

With reluctance, I turned away and rejoined the others. My search had come up flat, but it didn't matter. They were skiing in the direction they had scouted, which meant they had found a way.

An hour later, Woods and Tim stumbled onto the perfect camp. When I skied up to them, my excitement matched theirs. They were proud of this camp. Looking around, I didn't blame them. The melted out rock ledge was broad enough for a tent! By the time I was done gawking at the view, Adam's pack exploded across a 30-square-foot area.

He had food in hand, and he was barefoot. I laughed to myself—we don't call him the 'Adam bomb' for nothing!

Even with all this perfection, I thought of pushing the group on. Then I remembered the expression, "You're not Russian, so why you rushin'?"

When alpenglow washed the alpine in pink hues, I stood above the Hagen Glacier, far above camp. My skis were already on. They itched to turn. My last lap of the night laid in wait, curled up below me on a shoulder of glacier. As I dropped in, my edges bit into the snow. They smeared their teeth. With my body wrapped in gravity's fist, she hurled me down the slope, and I loved every second of it.

Nighttime arrived as my skis ascended to a pass. A

Above: Our route descended from the left skyline of North Despair. **Right:** View of Mt. Triumph.

Adam surmounts Mystery Ridge on our return to Berdeen Lake.

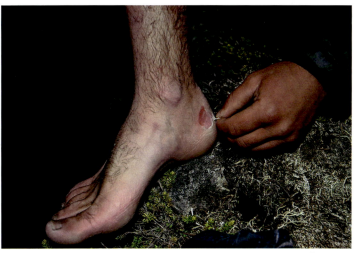
Foot gnar.

headlamp-assisted descent led back to our camp at 5900 feet. Exhausted, I lay in my tent with hot food. It was a simple pleasure, and an appreciated one.

June 6th: Bacon Peak

Rolling out of bed, I saw a narrow couloir that scarred the side of Hagen Peak. Adam and Tim insisted we ski it. While I reluctantly agreed, Woods decided that he'd rather get a jump on the day. I gave him directions and he set off. Afterward, Adam and Tim joined me in climbing Hagen Peak one final time.

An hour later, my heart pounded in my ears, and sweat drooled down my brow. It was a warm day for a climb. This was good for us since it would soften the snow on our objective.

From the top, I swept my first turns. More perfect, again. Too many days of perfect to handle! Snow splashed over cliffs, and the sunrays spider-webbed through that wave of snow as I looked back up the mountainside to watch the others, and to appreciate my tracks.

After skiing halfway down, I took my skis off. I found a stable seat atop a jutting ledge of rock that overlooked the couloir. From there, I filmed Adam skiing the lower half of the line. The rush of watching him from above was like fuel in my veins. That thrill pressed the pedal to the floor and jolted me to my feet and back to my skis.

The line was laid below Tim and me. It was beautiful. There's sweat equity in climbing what you ski. A satisfaction

Adam looking at Bacon Peak

Bacon Peak

Close-up of Bacon Peak

Green Lake

Above: The outlet of Berdeen Lake. **Right:** Our camp perched on rock ledges.

Woods snowboarding on the Hagan Glacier.

like you get when you build something with your own hands. I felt like I was putting the finishing touches on a cabinet I had built. Each turn was a layer of varnish or a sweep of sandpaper.

After skiing down, high fives and laughs were shared all around. Temporarily, we had forgotten about the work ahead. No matter, because it felt good to be tied to the moment.

Above a cauldron of water, with camp long ago taken down and packed, I linked patches of snow together as we continued our traverse to Bacon Peak. Adam and Tim made the sane decision and stuffed themselves between tight trees, eventually skiing onto open slopes below Nert Lake, unscathed. I came away with a few scratches, which is just the way I like it.

Adam and Tim rested at Nert Lake while I set off ahead of them. At the end of my second switchback, I stopped. Across the alpen slopes, cloud shadows played tag. My halting continued to the top of the first of two large hills that rose above Green Lake. The waters, now frozen, captivated me even more than the cloud shadows. Surrounding cliffs admonished my intrusion to either, but couldn't hinder my view. Silver water poured from their parapets.

Billowing white clouds floated in pools of deep blue overhead. Between was Bacon Peak and her coat of broad, gentle glaciers.

I caught Woods 1,000 feet below the summit of Bacon Peak (7,070 feet), and the others arrived shortly thereafter. Again, we weren't in a hurry. We stopped and pitched camp. When done, we each set off with our own ski objectives for the evening, and when satisfied, we returned, each in our own time.

As the sun took one final bow, Woods climbed a rocky ridge. He worked his way to a tower that rose at its end. His vantage offered unhindered views of Mount Baker. It didn't exactly reward better views than there were below, but there's something to be said for a throne. Woods stood atop

Taking the scenic route down Mt. Hagan.

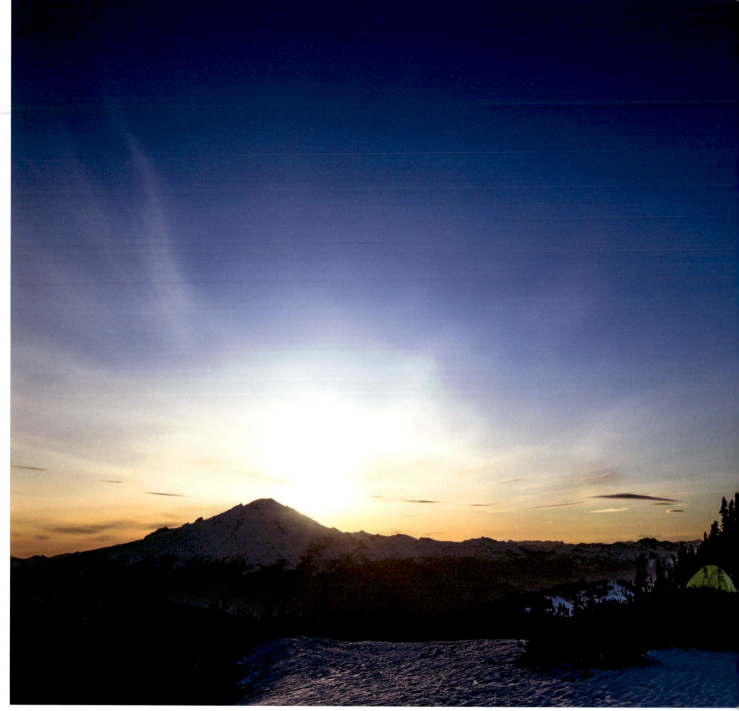

Woods at camp with Baker at sunset.

it and yelled at me, the sunset or the mountains—I don't know which. It was a carnal joy. It was pure and awesome. It called to my inner lion, and soon I roared with him—at nothing and everything.

June 7th: Watson Lakes Trailhead

We arrived on the summit of Bacon Peak before 9 AM. We didn't pause there long. The car and food pulled us forward, drawing us in toward promised comforts. In the time we did take there, the view toward Despair held all our attention. It appeared so far away. Among the other peaks, it is practically lost in the skyline. But now, we knew it; we found it in seconds.

Turning away, we skied toward a 6,400-foot notch cut onto the side of Bacon Peak's 1,500-foot Southwest Face.

On the descent, we leapfrogged each other down and around cliff bands, pockets of trees and bare patches. Eventually we arrived at a point where our skis had to be packed. Adam took the lead. He squealed and grunted depending on how secure the huckleberry bushes or fir tree branches proved to be. We bushwhacked 200 feet through steep terrain. Not bad, considering what we had done on our first day.

At the valley floor, the snow reappeared.

A circuitous mile took us to Diobsud Lakes. In the summer, it is a bug-ridden collection of ponds. In the spring, I feared those pestilent bugs were merely hidden just under the snow, readying to leap out and swarm all over me. As you can tell, I have bad memories of the place. On my last

View from the top.

Resting and refueling.

adventure here, a pound of flesh was carried away by those voracious flies! That can scar a man, and I'm not saying this lightly. I let a hundred mosquitoes bite, all at once, without so much as flinching.

It was only as my skis climbed away from the lakes that I appreciated them.

Over a few passes, up and around ridge lines, and then onto the Watson Glacier. By then, I was far ahead of the others. I stopped and pulled out my journal and wrote of the day. I drew a picture and cringed at my poor representation of my surrounding environment. Putting it away, I looked above me. The clouds were heavy, and rain would be coming soon. I took a few photos to pass the time. With this, at least, I have some artistic skill; although it doesn't take much to compete with stick figures.

Eventually, we descended a stream bed and arrived onto snow-covered forest roads. We glided 4 miles in a flurry of arms and legs. More often than not, no matter where you are in the Cascades, you are scooting down one road or another at the beginning or end of a trip. Consider it part of the Green Wall I mentioned earlier, and be thankful. This is wilderness, and it has every right to be inaccessible.

Our clothes and hair were a mess when we arrived at my car. None of us had shaved. Our clothes were muddied and stank. Put together, none of this could mask the straightening of our stance or glare in our eyes. There was something different in them. I don't know what, exactly, but it was there. We were changed for the better, and that's all that mattered.

Adam skiing Bacon Peak.

Above: Tim skiing a couloir on Hagan Peak. **Right:** Tim reflects on a week well spent.

Hours later, dulled by too much driving, I arrived home heavy-lidded. Even with sleep tugging at me as I climbed the stairs to my room, I couldn't help but pause at my maps. The first place I hunted out from the topo lines was Despair. Just as I had spotted the line on her slopes from Mount Degenhardt all those years ago, I spotted another from the top of North Despair. I knew its trajectory. With little effort, I located it on the maps, and I learned its name.

With a satisfied smile, I flicked my light off, slipped into bed and dreamed. Soon I was tightening boots, snapping on bindings and gliding downward. Even far from the mountains that are my church, I entered her cathedral, and she kept me there, twisted up in her arms. I grinned and concluded, "Maybe I'll stay a bit longer, just this once." ▲

The Alpine Oasis

A destination for mountain rejuvenation.

Boot tracks lead to Cache Col. North Cascades, Washington State.

Jessy Hummel hucking off The Doughnut. White Pass, Washington State.

Josh Hummel and Kyle Miller battling wind on the Coleman Glacier, Mt. Baker. North Cascades, Washington State.

Jessy Hummel ripping the tape off his mangled feet. North Cascades, Washington State.

Kyle Miller crossing Gold Creek. Alpine Lakes Wilderness, Washington State.

Kyle Miller's horde. Olympic National Park, Washington State.

Forest McBrian near the top of the Northwest Buttress of the Southwest peak of Bonanza.

Kyle Miller admiring Mt. Rainier, Washington State.

From left: Hannah Carrigan, Kyle Miller, Holly Walker and Adam Roberts do the snow dance. Garibaldi Park, Canada.

Hannah Carrigan crossing a creek at the base of the Paradise Glacier. Mt. Rainier, Washington State.

Andy Mahre flies off Hogsback. White Pass, Washington State.

Tom Murphy banking a turn on the Nisqually Glacier. Mt. Rainier, Washington State.

Jessy Hummel and Adam Roberts on the McAllister Glacier. North Cascades, Washington State.

Kyle Miller above stands above Pea Soup Lake. Alpine Lakes Wilderness, Washington State.

A blanket of clouds slumbers below Adam Roberts as he descends the steep pyramid on Mount Shuksan. North Cascades, Washington State

Between shaking knees, Ryan Lurie ascends the fightingly steep NW Face of Castle Towers. Garibaldi Park, British Columbia.

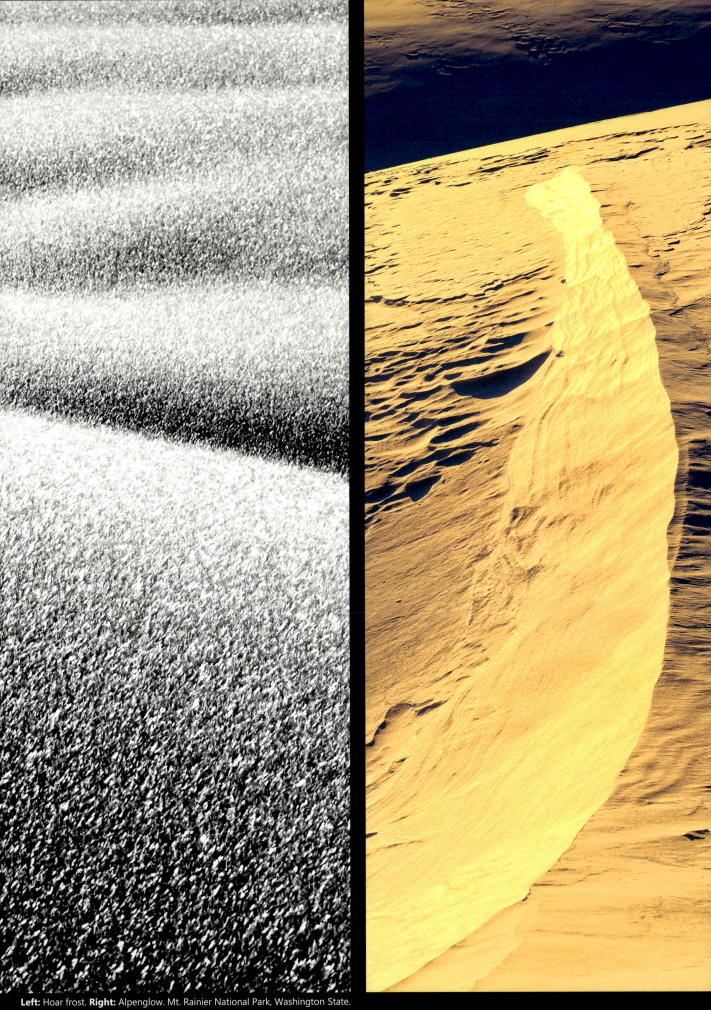

Left: Hoar frost. **Right:** Alpenglow. Mt. Rainier National Park, Washington State.

Cutting a skin track high on Shuksan Arm. North Cascades, Washington State.

Forbidden Peak as seen from the Inspiration Glacier. North Cascades, Washington State.

Jason Hummel, Kyle Miller and Brennan Van Loo on Bonanza Peak. North Cascades, Washington State.

Massive snow creeping on the Douglas Glacier, Mt. Logan. North Cascades, Washington State.

Sahale Mountain in Autumn as seen from the Inspiration Glacier. North Cascades, Washington State.

THE WHITE HEART

Traversing the Picket Range in Winter

The Picket Traverse | North Cascades National Park
Washington State, USA

"Where am I?" I wondered, once again awakening cold and shivering.

Looking up, I saw the specter of my nightmares—the Picket Range loomed overhead, beguiling me with her contours of ridge and slope. Answering my own question, sprinkled with obscenities, I tried to fall back asleep, sporadically waking over and again, each time grasping that I was indeed in the Pickets and scared as hell they'd keep me forever, entombed in moonlit fingers of snow and ice.

For six days, Forest and I would cross the Picket Range in North Cascade National Park from south to north: across Stetattle Ridge, down into McMillan Cirque, over Mount Fury, down into Luna Cirque, over Mount Challenger, down Perfect Pass, then out via the Mineral High Route to Hannegan Pass Road.

We would complete a high traverse of the Picket Range, in the middle of winter, crossing perhaps 50 miles of some of the most wild and remote mountains in the lower 48.

Monday morning, two days before the trip, I stared at an e-mail from a guy I didn't know. It said, "I'm headed to the Pickets for a ski traverse during the approaching high-pressure, and I'm looking for a partner." Forest McBrian

Carl Skoog standing among the North Cascades during the 1985 pioneering traverse of the Picket Range. *Photo by Lowell Skoog.*

turned out to be a single test away from becoming a fully certified AMGA guide. He would be one of only a handful in the entire country to receive all three certifications. Having completed his alpine and rock climbing disciplines, he had one remaining—ski mountaineering. After this trip, I could attest that he wouldn't have much difficulty passing.

In May 1985, Jens Kieler, along with brothers Carl and Lowell Skoog, pioneered a ski traverse through the esoteric Picket Range. They would be the inspiration for our trip. In the quarter century since, to their knowledge, no one had repeated this impressive feat. You can read more about their

Mountain, where beat poet Gary Snyder spent the summer of 1953 as a fire lookout. His story, among others, is featured in the book, *Poets on the Peaks*.

As we reached snow, put on our skins and continued to where we could peer over the top of Stetattle Ridge, I could understand why these vistas inspired poetry. Their fire and brimstone gathers up your breath and steals it away, sheltering you with only their shadows.

As I neared the heart of the range, I became lost in the hike up and down ridge after ridge. When I look into these mountains I see not only peaks of rock and ice, but arms

Forest McBrian on Sourdough Ridge.

adventure in the 1986 article Lowell wrote for *Rock and Ice Magazine*. Lowell says near the conclusion of his article, "… As we plodded slowly down the steep trail to Diablo, our legs were wobbly, our hands and faces sunburned, and our feet aching. But our mountain souls were soaring. We had skied the Pickets, and in so doing had found the climax of the North Cascade high routes." My hope was that our mountain souls would also soar and stay aloft through any number of failures that could beset us and force an early retreat.

Leaving Diablo Lake, at 900 feet, with skis and boots, overnight gear, and a healthy dose of optimism, Forest and I, joined by Kyle Miller, climbed through thick woods along a steep, winding trail to Stetattle Ridge, near Sourdough

and legs, torsos and heads. It becomes so intertwined that, like a den of snakes, where one mountain begins another peeks out. Within this tightly bound range, stretching a mere six miles in length, there are at least 21 summits over 7,500 feet high.

As I carved out my bed from the snow and set up my bivy on my first day, I could only think about getting closer to these mountains, curling up in her arms and losing myself in that convolution of alpine grandeur. I've seen no place more seductive than the Picket Range.

In the following day and a half, feet and skis reached forward, and then pulled back … forward and back, over and again. Terrain rolled away before eyes. Overhead, beneath

MCMILLAN SPIRES

Spines and ridge lines awash in aplenglow.

Above: Fluted slopes above Azure lake. **From top:** Elephant Butte; Kyle Miller; Forest McBrian and McMillan Spires; Ridge line above Azure Lake.

McMillan Spires, a spine of rock and snow bristled with trees. It's amazing where a tree will gain purchase. There was no better example of this tenacity than in the depths of the North Cascades where avalanches, ice falls and glaciers encroach on every aspect. It certainly proves that where life has a will, there is always a way.

Night grew out of shadows and crawled up from the valleys, cornering us in our bivy sacks. Or, as I joked to Kyle, "our ice coffins." Stoves roared and cooking persisted for an hour. Stars tumbled from the moon's glow as the night went

on and on and on—longer than a man can sleep.

Early morning, on our third day, brought warmth, as our bodies began to move. A few hours of work, and we gazed into McMillan Creek Cirque, our three brains firing off—dismantling confidence with the same ire of a bomb specialist in the midst of disarming a potentially destructive device. Our thoughts rang in a similar note: "Oh my God, if I go down there, I am committed!" This was the bomb in the closet: red or green wire? Five, four, three, two and CUT. Then the countdown shuttered to a stop. Kyle found conditions

too risky, especially after a small slide nearly swallowed him the day before.

Midday on the third day of our trip, Forest and I bid farewell to Kyle as he turned back the way we had come. Those goodbyes only took a moment. I looked around one last time, and he was gone. We knew he could return safely by staying on the ridge crest. He agreed and, selfishly, Forest and I continued. We both felt guilty for the remainder of the trip.

Looking ahead I knew, "I must get closer!" We were so close now, I felt the cold breath of wind sucking us in.

The question remained, teetering in my thoughts, would we be swallowed, or would we be the mice that got the cheese and got away to cheese hunt another day?

The edge of McMillan Creek Cirque, where we were perched, is dominated by cornices. They reached over the shadowed confines of this massive valley. Their unknown challenges sprinkled throughout. Forest dropped in, and with a push, I followed. My worries wouldn't recede. I imagined being stranded by foul weather and left with no option, other than resorting to days of retreat through jungle corridors. It rankled our self-assurance. Yet, uncertainty is the great mediator. It unclogs the moment and asserts her presence, with each turn downward, from the untenable slurry of responsibility.

With the north cirque walls an hour behind us, all looming and dominating, the sun broke out from behind Mount Terror and splashed the valley with its allotted few hours of precious light. Our gear scattered on warmed rocks, next to a gurgling stream. Boots came off and not much was said. The path ahead, over Mount Fury, would be across warming south faces. Climbing them would have to wait for colder temperatures the following day.

Satisfied, I pulled up a bottle of clean, crisp water and soaked in the sunlight. Bathing in it, my worries scattered.

"It's time," Forest mumbled. He knew I was already awake. Slipping from my sleeping bag, I left my dreamy distractions behind and submitted myself to the biting morning cold of our fourth day.

In May 1985, Skoog and party climbed over Outrigger Peak on their way between McMillan Cirque and Luna Cirque. A direct route made more sense in winter, so we began by ascending through trees to a place marked 'waterfall' on the map, which jolted laughter from us; how many

Our descent into McMillan Cirque.

Outrigger Peak

receive no mention at all? Without a rope, we wondered, could we climb over? The answer was an ecstatic *yes*!

Upper snowfields passed by in a blink. Telltale signs of softening snow weren't visible yet, but Forest pressed me, asking, "Do you want to climb Fury?" My concern of warming temperatures and potential avalanches convinced me to say *no*!

The descent from the shoulder of Mount Fury brought us into a tiny cirque that we could then climb to Luna-Fury Col. Between cornices, the descent was laced with powder and wind board. To us, this was unbottled perfection. It carpeted the entire slope, all the way down to the bottom, where I transitioned to uphill mode and followed Forest on a high traverse, all smiles. We quickly climbed until we could see into Luna Creek Cirque. It was blanketed in more powder and sprinkled with trees. Their green lines climbed valley walls like ants from their nest.

Before we left, Forest, between bites of cheese, foretold quite matter-of-factly, "These will be the best turns of my life." As we descended into Luna Creek Cirque, I couldn't help but think how right he was.

In an hour, we skied deep into the bowels beneath the North Face of Mount Fury. Through there, we climbed over avalanche debris for hours before finding escape onto the friendlier Challenger Glacier.

We arrived at camp after an 8,000-foot day of climbing.

Gearing up for an ascent of Mt. Fury.

Above: Crossing avalanche debris. **Below:** Himmelgeisterhorn

Above: Unexpected powder. **From top:** Leaving Luna-Fury Col.; at the base of McMillan Cirque; pow lines near the SE face of Mt. Fury; Forest McBrian.

Spent legs pushed me the final bit. As I flattened out a small bivy spot, I made sure I'd have excellent views of the Northeast Face of Mount Fury.

Seven years ago, I skied the Northeast Face of Mount Fury in very poor late season conditions with excellent friends; it was one of the scariest descents of my life.

As night blossomed, I flattened out an area for my camera and with numbed fingers I spent an hour trying to get 'the shot' just the way I wanted—a mountain's restless night—and I believe I succeeded.

A fifth morning reminded me that it's winter. Every morning made a point of doing so. Stuffed like a taco in my bag, between shivers I laughed, "How can I be warm and freezing at the same time?" I could have done without those awfully long nights, but as in everything, including mountains, there is a price of entry. To be here, a spectator to such a place, some discomfort is required. Would I want it any different?

An hour later, we climbed over the broad shoulder of Mount Challenger. It is the southernmost peak in the range. From it, the core of the Picket Range receded from

Finding solitude on Luna Lake.

view, and before I left it behind, I paused. Some consider these mountains the wildest in the lower 48. Comparisons are like men rating woman. We'll never agree. At that moment, as these peaks gazed back at me, I knew one thing for sure: I realized how cultivated and tame I am compared to this place!

Creaking, my skis continued their journey forward.

Names in the Pickets suit the terrain so well that, beyond them, little description is needed. We left the Challenger Glacier behind, crossed over Perfect Pass and finagled our way beyond Imperfect Impasse to the laid back contours of Easy Ridge.

Farther along, a choice: We could drop to the Chilliwack Trail or continue on the Mineral Mountain High Route. Since staying high had purified us, the only reason we would descend to the lowlands was clouds. They'd have to infect the all-encompassing blue sky. So far, not a germ of white puffiness was in sight, so gallivanting like Dorothy and her friends down the yellow brick road, off to the Mineral Mountain High Route we went.

Story continued on Page 142

The Northeast Face of Mount Fury

By Ben Manfredi

Ben Manfredi on the summit of Luna Peak. *Photo by Jason Hummel.*

Editor's Note: This is an excerpt from Day 3 on the Northeast Face of Mt. Fury, June 16, 2003.

It seems we reached the summit around 11am. The sun had graced portions of the Northeast Face but the majority needed more time to allow our edges grip. How long, we weren't certain but with nearly 10 hours of daylight remaining, the longer, the better.

The summit was an extraordinary haven with peerless views in every direction. My only regret was not being able to see ourselves because we stood atop the granddaddy of them all. Beckey writes, "Mt. Fury epitomizes the grand alpine wilderness of the amazing Picket Range." I'm bound to agree.

There was no wind on the summit but it was covered in snow. I decided to make the most of my 1-2 hours there by taking a nap and some cozy rocks to the west provided the perfect loft -- the kind you get all teary-eyed and empty-stomach just thinking about. I took off my boots to dry my socks and fixed a ham and cheese sandwich complete with mustard and mayo. Some chewy shock tarts did me in and for the next hour, I was in heaven.

By noon the mountains had restored my energy so I got dressed to see what Jason [Hummel] and Sky [Sjue] were up to. I found them sprawled across the snowy summit making use of their packs to stay dry. Besides sun, the only weather we had to shelter was the cloud of BS that engulfed us from the start. The summit showers were particularly heavy. At one point I even sought my cell phone to call Josh [Hummel] and proclaim our success. Looking down the Northeast Face provided a reality check and the showers subsided as the moment of truth approached.

Some serious talk got us to thinking that another summit of Fury the next day wasn't likely. Instead, we agreed to allow the final two days to backtrack our approach. A pick-up time of 6 PM at Ross Lake seemed too late so I called the resort and bumped it up to 2 PM.

Okay, so you've waited long enough and we've waited even longer so how about the ski.

By noon we were getting antsy and by 1 PM our hair must have been standing on end. The smooth slope was still

Jason Hummel ascending the Northeast Face of Fury, far above Lousy Lake. *Photo by Ben Manfredi.*

The Northeast Face of Fury, from the summit of Mt. Challenger. *Photo by Ben Manfredi.*

firm but the lower runnels had been getting plenty of sun and that was our main concern. We wanted them soft but not too soft. What we really wanted was to get it over with and now seemed like as good of time as any.

I took the role of photographer so Sky agreed to go first. A cautious set of turns led him through the smooth slope and left beneath some rocks to the start of the runnels. Jason went next stopping midway to let me pass. The Southeast Glacier became even more tempting after chattering my way down 50-degree ice. The smooth slope was no softer than a baby's toenail. Fortunately, the start of the runnels provided some breakable crust that I could tell would turn to mush at any moment. I stopped there and kicked a platform for a photo of Jason.

OK, I'm getting sweaty just thinking about it but I digress. The least of our concerns was over. How about them runnels? I called down to Sky and we seemed to agree that left of center looked best. There were two problems with this route. First, we weren't sure that we could ski it. Second, we would need to cross the main runnel at some point to get back to skier's right as it provided the only route down the lower face. The only problem with right of center (the way we climbed) was that we were pretty sure we couldn't ski it. We don't normally choose the route with more problems but in this case it was worth the gamble.

The breakable crust was very unpredictable so we ended up taking turns skiing inside the main runnel until its sides became too steep and icy to surmount. A bobsled might have kept going but we had no desire to become a luge so after a couple hundred feet, we exited left.

Our next move was uncertain as the slope narrowed between the main runnel and a rock spur on the left. I led some pleasant turns before traversing left to cross more runnels and more unpleasant turns. I called it quits above the narrow slope and found myself sidestepping the sloppy 60-degree crux with half a ski length to edge. Loose it and you join the rock, snow, ice, and every other piece of debris inside the rift. It took all my focus, most of my patience, and a good deal of my energy before rounding the corner to safety.

Sky wasn't too far behind. He started the next slope while I waited for Jason.

The next set of turns ended at a large runnel that entered from the left. Sky's first impression was that we'd have to downclimb but I yelled some free-heel encouragement and he somehow managed. From there we had to join the main runnel at the edge of oblivion and after a few tense sidesteps it was over.

Finally, the end of the upper face. We took our skis off and discovered a sizable cliff below us. This gave us a good look at the lower face which offered more cliffs, more runnels,

Above: Jason Hummel and the Southern Pickets. **Right:** Jason Hummel descending the Northeast Face. Below: The boat ride on Ross Lake. *Photos by Ben Manfredi.*

and a few crevasses. There was a clear route through the runnels and crevasses but no apparent exit through the final cliff. I had a sinking suspicion that we might get cut off ever since my view from Challenger the previous week. We faced a short climb to skier's right so I figured we ought to just continue to our tracks and descend the Fury Glacier. Paper, rock, scissors… watch it! A basketball-size rock came tumbling from high above into the rift and over the cliff suggesting that our decision time had passed and that the lower face was out of the question.

With skis on pack and UTBs on foot I hurried up, across, and out of the main runnel. Sky and Jason met up with me in a crevasse that we tried to milk for water. This was just below the 'schrund that we passed beneath that morning so it wasn't long before we reached the saddle. I had some second thoughts but they were quickly forgotten as the ski down the Fury Glacier provided much better turns than lower face appeared to. We took one wrong turn at the beginning of the ice fall with the hope of going center. Skier's right provided the only alternative. I stopped for water above a cliff before descending to Luna Lake. From there we traversed its northern shore to a rock outcropping where we rested.

I wasn't looking forward to climbing back to the col but knew it was my duty to break track. Sky carried the rope and led the upper slope of the Northeast Face. Jason carried too

much food and spent too much time trying to eat it. In all actuality, I was on a mission. Having gotten to camp past 9 PM the previous two days I was looking forward to an early dinner and some much-needed rest.

With one last photo I was off. The others stopped a couple hundred feet below so they didn't actually know what was going on inside my twisted head. There was no rush to join me so I think we understood each other.

My only rest came halfway up where I stopped for water among the bountiful streams. I reached camp around 7 PM.

With so much food at camp I felt obliged to pillage. By the time the others arrived I was well on my way through a second sandwich and dessert.

We went to bed with full stomachs, bloated minds, and plenty of daylight. A fitting end to a gut-wrenching day.

With no alarms, a dark tent, and 0-degree sleeping bag, the only thing that would be waking me was warmth. The sun broke free from Luna's shadow around 7am and I awoke shortly after. We basked on the rocks for upwards of an hour and spent another hour packing. At the col we discovered our tracks had nearly melted and realized that our turns from the previous day would soon be gone. I turned my back with an exclamation. "My work here is done!" Deep down I knew that wasn't the case but it still felt good to say.

We bid farewell to Mount Fury. Until next time.

Story continued from Page 133

An 1,800-foot climb took an hour and ten minutes. This was the easy part. Our descent took much longer. Like so many Cascade mountains, the biggest challenges often lay hidden deep in the valleys, nestled as a viper in the grass, waiting to strike.

Fangs of cliff on Mineral Mountain's northwest face forced us to sidestep treacherous terrain, each turn committing us further. "Forest, have you found a way?" I croaked, seeing nothing myself. He eventually called out, thankfully offering relief, "Stay high!" In front of me, a small couloir, as wide as my skis, granted passageway to the slopes below, and to Chilliwack Pass. We decided to spend our final night there.

Day six brought us from forests to the upper slopes of Ruth Mountain. The sun greeted us as we climbed out from the shady, powder-filled slopes onto the sunlit landscapes that rolled away ahead of us. Eventually, the traversing ended as we rounded Ruth's west face.

In the cold breeze, we ate our remaining scraps of food. Neither of us felt hurried, both knowing that this was it—soon our journey would be over. Submitting to it, I mumbled, "We should go." How soon, I knew, we'd be back to cars, roads, cities, towns, beds, warmth, and food—*the easy life*. I didn't need a mirror to know we looked haggard, sun-burnt and beat. While it's good to not have creature comforts all the time, you certainly need them some of the time.

An hour later, my skis shuddered to a stop on a rock-strewn trail, under a forest canopy bereft of snow. In minutes, those skis were laid on weary shoulders as I hiked the last of the trail to the Hannegan Pass Road. While skis can't be weary or tired, I think they joined me in my backward glances. We were done. We were no longer racing uninhibited from the firm grip of the unforgiving Picket Range. And, unlike Forest just ahead of me, my skis were unafraid. No matter how often I visit, I would always awaken fearful of these mountains. To me that's what makes them so extraordinary. ⋀⋀

Skiing above Chilliwack Pass.

#livelikeliz

By Davide De Masi

Liz Daley wearing her ever-present smile. Mt. Baker, Washington State.

On the 29th of September, 29-year-old Liz Daley, a professional splitboarder and mountain guide based out of Seattle, Washington, was lost to an avalanche near El Chalten, Argentina, on a snowboard/ski-mountaineering expedition. Liz snowboarded and guided in Alaska and the North Cascades and was frequently based out of Chamonix, France.

Liz's physical and mental transformation from a mountain enthusiast of humble beginnings to a respected leader in the mountain community happened in the blink of an eye. Her dreamy smile and flowing blond hair embodied her down-home spirit as that girl from Tacoma, but with an iron core of adept mountain sense, experience and raw talent for mountain sports. Liz brought beauty to beautiful places and instilled a natural a sense of femininity in the most masculine of environments. Her unique sense of stoke and girliness was unmistakable and immediately accessible to everyone. Liz brought the party to the mountains.

Her inspirational voyage was so remarkably terminated at its absolute peak that we can only wonder where her trajectory would have brought her. In the same sense, to us she was perfectly preserved at the pinnacle of her life.

She was still blissful from our recent engagement party days before her departure on her dream expedition with our best friend, Drew Tabke. Her final days were filled with life, wonderment and light. Her lasting image to us will be her vivacious smile, backed by her tenacious and splendid amazement and deep anticipation for the future.

Anyone that met Liz—no matter how briefly—has a good indication of how she shared this precious and elusive gift of genuine love. Her innate accepting and caring nature was immediately apparent to anyone, whether it be a new acquaintance or her future husband. Liz was always able to look beyond the temporary obstacles that we create for ourselves and generate a realistic, optimistic and passionate image of the future. Liz had a remarkable ability to subconsciously draw from deep within her core values of love and inspiration and shape her relationships and goals even during the darkest moments. Her ability to manifest her relentless love for life and cultivate herself into a remarkable and capable partner, friend and professional will motivate us for the rest of our lives.

[**Editor's Note:** Davide De Masi was the fiancé of Liz Daley.]